MULTIPLE LIVES

'Born with the gift of laughter, and a sense that the world was mad.'

Rafael Sabatini

'Your insight is clear and unbiased,' said the gracious Sovereign, 'But however entrancing it is to wander unchecked through a garden of bright images, are we not enticing your mind from another subject of equal importance?'

From *Kai Lung Unrolls His Mate*
by Ernest Bramah

MULTIPLE LIVES

The Autobiography of
JOANNA GREENLAW

Go thy way with brow serene,
Fear not thy simple tale to tell,
The whisper of the Desert Wind,
The tinkle of the camel's bell.

The Kasidah
by Sir Richard Burton

CYHOEDDWYR DINEFWR PUBLISHERS

Copyright © 2004 Joanna Greenlaw

Published in 2004 by
Cyhoeddwyr Dinefwr Publishers
Rawlings Road, Llandybie
Carmarthenshire, SA18 3YD

The right of Joanna Greenlaw to be identified as the Author
of the Work has been asserted by her in accordance with
the Copyright, Designs and Patents Act 1988.

*All rights reserved. No part of this publication may be reproduced,
stored in a retrieval system or transmitted, in any form or by any
means without the prior permission of the publisher,
nor be otherwise circulated in any form of binding or cover
other than that in which it is published and without similar
condition being imposed on the subsequent purchaser.*

A CIP catalogue record for this book is
available from the British Library.

ISBN 1-904323-07-3

Printed and bound in Wales by
Dinefwr Press Ltd.
Rawlings Road, Llandybie
Carmarthenshire, SA18 3YD

CONTENTS

Foreword	6
Introduction	7
An Edwardian Pygmalion and a fractious Galatea	9
Marionettes and Painted Carts. A childhood in the land of the Godfathers	20
My India	26
Palaces, Forts, Dacoits, and manic drivers. A drive through India from Bombay to Kashmir	42
Mammy-wagons, Snakes, and the Dark Continent. West Africa in 1957	51
Arabs, Kasbahs, and *Vin Ordinaire*. North Africa, as seen from the sea	58
Convoys, U-Boats, and learning to play stud poker	67
The Brief-Case Years	71
Cows and Muck-Heaps – Two Years Hard Labour	84
The Wonderful Sea charmed me from the First	88
The Smile on the Face of Giaconda. The Labyrinth of Gender	97
Pampas, Tangos, and Steaks which overhung the Plate. Buenos Aires, 1946 and 1976	108
Clocks, Ships, and Writing. 'Well, Mr Gibbon, still scribble, scribble, scribble?' (William IV on meeting Edward Gibbon)	114
Index	124

FOREWORD

It is some years since I was privileged to make the acquaintance of Joanna Greenlaw. Her reputation as a magician with grandfather clocks caused me to invite her to my home to examine an old Llandeilo-made clock inherited through several generations of my wife's family. It had stood silent and reproachful in our hall for many years. In less than two minutes Joanna brought it to life!

Since then Joanna has 'brought to life', through her previous books, some of her own fascinating experiences and given us an insight into two unique areas of British Maritime History. It was my pleasure to be somewhat involved in the launch of both *The Swansea Copper Barques and Cape Horners* and *The History of the Radio Officer in the British Merchant Navy and on Deep-Sea Trawlers*.

At our first meeting we discovered a mutual interest in the sea which has played a large part in Joanna's life, and now I am honoured to have been asked to write this foreword to Joanna's autobiography. Perhaps it has something to do with the fact that we share the same birthday date of May 24th – Empire Day.

Joanna hails from the same generation as me. Spanning the still great but declining years of the British Empire, through a World War and many conflicts since, to an age which would have been unrecognisable to our parents' generation and which has many features which my generation and Joanna's find disturbing and difficult to accept.

We dismiss at our peril the values and behaviour which are a constant thread through Joanna's autobiography.

Her book spans a spectrum of life that is both compelling and fascinating. It gives us an insight into a way of life never to be repeated and crosses many borders of experience and adventure.

I congratulate Joanna on her willingness to be so open about her life and so frank in her views. I thank her for sharing with us her exciting moments, and her high points and low points in what has been, so far, an extraordinary story.

"*Life is a dream, and it is well that it is so, or who could survive some of its experiences.*" (Isadora Duncan, 1877-1927).

COMMODORE R. C. HASTIE, CBE, RNR

INTRODUCTION

IN WRITING THIS BOOK I had originally planned to revisit in memory countries and places which had formed the background to the main events of my life, and attempt perhaps to interpret their meaning. But the list, as I drew it up, became ever longer, extending over a large part of the world, and I realised there was a danger of creating a monster volume – boring as a politician's memoirs – with the honourable exception of the late Alan Clark.

Instead, I have chosen certain themes and locations that have particularly interested me, and incidentally lend themselves to treatment in the light of my own experience at the time. The most important are: India under the British Raj; the Merchant Navy, which I joined in 1942; the Arab countries which fringe the Mediterranean, including the Middle East, and an unreal period I have christened the 'Brief-Case Years'. I have also reflected on the subject of gender, triggered by my own change of *modus operandi*, which took place more than twenty years ago.

The title of this book did not come upon me as a spontaneous piece of inspired creativity. Instead, it crept up silently as I realised that in each stage of my life I have been playing no more than the part required by that particular scenario. Born under the fatal sign of Gemini, from birth as restless as a baby snake, never happy unless trying to keep six balls in the air at the same time, how could it be otherwise?

I was born on the 24th of May, 1925, Empire Day, the first of many jokes played on me by jesting fortune. In the West it is called Fate and in the East, Kismet, but I believe that at birth something is bound about our brow that we cannot evade. Nowadays, Empire Day does not even appear in the dictionary, so far removed are we from my childhood, when a quarter of the globe was ruled from London, and a British passport was still a document viewed with respect once one had crossed the Channel. It foreshadowed a childhood spent in northern India under the British Raj, which then seemed to me as immutable as the Pyramids, although it had only another two decades to run.

Since then the mysterious workings of Providence have taken me, working, travelling, and visiting, to most of the countries of the old British

Empire, and no-one will ever again see them as did I and my generation. I seem to remember that in 1935, when something must have brought my parents back to England for a brief interval (all their stays anywhere were short), I, in common with all other children, received a small oblong free Coronation box of chocolates with a picture of the King-Emperor, embellished with G. A. Henty-type crossed flags.

Perhaps it was foretold and summed up by the coloured repoussé map of the world on the lid of a large biscuit tin, which was my most treasured possession as a child.

There are deliberate gaps, mostly of a personal nature, and relating to others, for which I make no apology, for they are not part of my concept of the book. It has helped me to sort out things in my mind which have long needed clarifying, and if anyone else is interested I must regard that as a bonus. Originally, it was my intention to have it printed privately in a very limited edition, but events, as they have a habit of doing, have made me change my mind. It now remains for me to see what lies ahead, and I reflect that our greatest blessing is that we cannot know. It was Kipling who said: 'And nothing is saved of the trouble in store, for those who go down the road to Endor'.

Chapter 1

AN EDWARDIAN PYGMALION AND A FRACTIOUS GALATEA

BEFORE ME AS I write is a collection of objects redolent of the Edwardian era which I found among my father's effects when he died in 1946. There is a silver-mounted leather cigar-case consisting of two halves which fit together, and a hundred years later still shine exactly like a newly-opened conker, a small shark-skin covered case containing a silver monogram sealing set complete with red sealing wax and the letter S.V.L., an autograph book bound in soft leather with thick pastel coloured pages filled with entries which seem to have been made along the Baedekker trail all over Europe, a pile of old photographs and postcards, and several filled passports.

Holding the cigar-case in my hand, I think I can catch the authentic whiff of pre-World War I London, and hear the rattle of hansom cabs filled with Edwardian clubmen, and the sound of early motor-cars back-firing in Leicester Square.

My father once told me that he never felt dressed in London unless that cigar-case was full and there was an ample supply of the old white ten pound notes in his note-case. (He had never heard of a wallet, just as he became mystified when people talked about a room called a lounge.)

It was the London of the Café Royal with its gilded mirrors, and the Haute Bohême was in full swing; a mythical era glamourised by novelists like Michael Arlen, the Armenian magician, who in his books transformed London into an enchanted city, as full of adventure and romance as Shahrazad's City of the Caliphs.

My father was born in 1880 and joined the Indian Civil Service in 1902. A figure out of Kipling, rather than *Jewel and the Crown*, and such can be the contraction of historical time by extended lives, that I heard from him a second hand account of the Indian Mutiny in 1857, as he heard it from his father, who at the time carried on a fashionable medical practice in Calcutta.

He never read newspapers, believing they were all lies, and I was brought up with that salutary advice before me – an opinion I still regard as even more valid today. His other advice, and he wasn't joking, was to do no more than four hours work in any one day. After that the quality of one's output drastically falls, and you would be better employed in doing something else. Of course, he was right, and this fatal concept took a firm root, where it has complicated my life ever since.

Fortunately, I have able to get around it, by accepting my inherent low threshold of boredom, and always working in short bursts on different things. This approach received a firm grounding because I did not go to school until I was nearly eleven, my childhood being spent accompanying my parents as my father moved restlessly from one rented house to another in India and various parts of Europe.

I was taught to read by my mother with the aid of a chocolate alphabet, and did the rest myself, largely from Arthur Mee's *Children's Encyclopaedia*. I never played with any other children, and was so terrified of strangers that by the age of twelve I possessed as good a collection of phobias and complexes as ever filled the pockets of a Harley Street psychiatrist.

Only now do I realise how fortunate I was to escape the early stages of a standard education. I was free to learn at my own pace and read only about things that interested me. I was not confused by religious instruction, and free to read any of the books contained in the large wooden box which was always included in the mountain of trunks, suitcases, and hat-boxes that accompanied us on our travels. There were books on prehistoric animals, Norse and Greek mythology, Grimm's Fairy Tales, illustrated by Arthur Rackham, and Hans Anderson's by

Heath Robinson, and of course Robert Louis Stevenson. I looked at the illustrations in these books long before I could read them, which made me want to learn to read them, and explains why they are ingrained in my memory. What better background could there be to a child's mind than the tales of Jason and the Argonauts, Odysseus, and Odin, the one-eyed Norse king, who was God of the Wind, War, Magic. And then there was Artemis, Mistress of the Underworld, the Huntress, and the Goddess of Moon and Light, always attended by her pack of hunting dogs.

I did in fact briefly attend a village school in Pentewan, in Cornwall, when I was seven years old. It was during one of my father's brief spells in the UK and he had rented a small cottage on the hillside overlooking the little harbour. It was lit by oil-lamps and my chief recollection is of his lunch-time visits to the village alehouse and returning home in a state of alcoholic bad temper. It was only in after years that I discovered it had been occasioned by England going off the gold-standard, in the course of which he lost half his capital. In 1921, when he retired from the Indian Civil Service, he had returned to England with £80,000, a tidy sum in those days. When the crisis arose, it was a question of hanging on or selling out. I don't know which path he followed, but he was left in what he considered to be 'reduced circumstances'.

I think my presence at the school was an idea of my mother's; perhaps to get me out of the house and away from their continual quarrelling, when they sometimes came to blows. Whatever the reason, I found myself each morning deposited outside the village school and left to enter on my own into a large room where several stages of education were being conducted simultaneously. I had difficulty in understanding the local dialect, while for their part, my fellow pupils shrieked with laughter every time I opened my mouth; indeed, whenever I first appeared, they followed me around mimicking my accent. I felt that I had fallen among the children of barbarians, and feared for my safety.

Perhaps the only thing worth recalling about this depressing interlude is that one day the village idiot got run over by a steam-roller just outside the school, and reduced to the thickness of a pancake! Eventually, my mother tired of the scene I created every morning when I was deposited at the school gate, and my period of torture came to an end.

But it is time that I returned to Empire Day, 1925. Four months later, I was extracted from the care of the London Adoption Society by my adoptive parents; an event I did not learn of until my father's death in 1946, together with the interesting information that they had never married.

My father retired early from the Indian Civil Service after barely surviving an attack of black-water fever in Burma. It would seem from the memorabilia of this period of his life – which I found after his death – he had spent the interval between foot-loose and fancy-free along the Baedekker trail. But even before that his autograph book, in which the first entry was made by him on 13th September, 1910, covers the same sort of ground during leaves spent in England. (Scotland never appears, probably because he viewed the land of mist, heather and tossing the caber rather in the same light as Dr Johnson.)

That first entry, written by himself, haunts me, but I like to think that perhaps he wrote it in a passing moment of alcoholic depression between the lady friends:

> Better by far than a marble tomb,
> Than a monument over my head,
> (For what shall I care in my quiet room,
> for Headboard or Footboard when I am dead?)
> Better than glory or honours or fame,
> Though I am striving for those today,
> To know that some heart would cherish my name;
> And think of me kindly, with blessings, always.

It is the poignant confession of an essentially lonely man, and I did not understand until after his death that his life was a search for a happiness he never found. And I believe the explanation lies among the pile of old sepia photographs I found among my mother's papers after her death in Devon.

There is a portrait of him, probably taken when he was in his early thirties, against the usual Edwardian background of aspidestras and classical urns, mounted on thick yellowing cardboard. Only half of the original is left because it has been cut down the middle. On the right hand side appears the tantalising glimpse of the edge of an Edwardian flowered hat, and corresponding to it at the bottom, is the hem of a long dress. They are all that remain in the picture of his first wife, and the story he told me about her on one of our last walks before he died might have come straight from the lips of Mrs Hauksbee, whose ear for scandal and sharp tongue made her the terror of Simla society. It seems that she left him a few years after their marriage, taking with her exactly half of a large sum of money in a joint bank account, which she used to pay off the gambling and racing debts of her brother, an officer in the Indian army, to save him from being cashiered. My mother mentioned a name, which was that of a distinguished army family, but I do not give it here; such scandals are best left where they belong – in the past.

Until I went to sea in 1942, my father – unless he had been drinking – was a jovial, rather remote figure, always kind, but whose conversation with me largely consisted of jokes I could not understand. Sometimes he would return home with an extravagant yet almost useless present, such as a top-of-the-range Hornby clockwork engine but with no rails or carriages to go with it.

But on my first leave from sea things changed dramatically, and I cherish the memory of his delight when I first went with him to a pub for a drink Not long previously, in the course of his eternal moves, he had bought a house in Stafford after moving from a cottage in Pilton in North Devon. By an extraordinary coincidence who should I meet in the pub but the Second Mate of the *Ocean Viscount*, my first ship. His name was Lloyd Imber and in the unlikely event that these lines ever enter his field of vision, I send to him my hearty greetings across the years.

Among my father's old tinted postcards is one of a circular pergola on a promontory overlooking a fabulous view of the distant Himalayas, and labelled by him in faded ink 'Scandal

Point'. I like to believe that perhaps this is where father first fell in love with his first wife, Dolly. Looking back over more than fifty years, I now realise that he brooded over her desertion for the rest of his life and it created a gap that my mother was sadly never able to fill. It is now all best left with Mrs Hauksbee, along with the jinrickshaws and sola topis of British administrators who went up to Simla to escape summer on the plains.

The next entry in the autograph book is by Maud Tring, and is dated 14th September, 1910. It reads:

> Life is too short for aught
> But high endeavour;
> Too short for spite – but long enough for love.

Another by Constance Montgomery, 15th July, 1913:

> Full many a shaft at random sent,
> Finds a mark the archer little meant,
> And many a word at random spoken,
> May sooth or wound a heart that's broken.

There are so many of them, but the one I like best was by Lily Raven, London, 1916:

> The sunlight in the garden,
> Hardens and grows cold,
> And we cannot cage the minute,
> Within its net of gold.

Looking at what my father's lady friends wrote on the thick pastel-coloured pages of his autograph book, and the beautiful drawings which accompany some of the entries, I like to think that they were beautiful and kind and witty, and that somehow those enchanted moments remain forever in some magic time capsule which might one day might be revisited by those whose thoughts are captured in that little book, bound in the softest of red leather.

My mother and he came from completely different backgrounds, and while I think she was just as intelligent, they existed on disparate planes, if not planets. They quarrelled incessantly, sometimes coming to blows, and my childhood is full of memories of hiding under the bedclothes with my fingers in my ears to shut out the sound of their discord. For some reason trouble always reached its peak on an occasion like my birthday, or a visit to a zoo, or – worst of all – Christmas Day.

My father's regular habit was to go for a solitary walk in the morning which ended by calling in for a mid-day drink on the way home. It meant that he was often late for lunch, which triggered off another row. The horrific period in Pentewan was compounded by my humiliation when the village children jeeringly informed me that my father had been drunk in the local pothouse and had been asked to leave.

I have a good idea how these incidents cropped up. He would at first join in affably with the other lunch-time imbibers, and get into a discussion which led to an argument. He would then survey his surroundings and the company with distaste and become patronisingly offensive.

It is surprising that my parents managed to stay together for twenty-one years. I can only assume that they needed each other to argue with, and both felt a duty to me. The manner of their meeting accorded with the tragi-comedy of their life together, for it took place at a Lyon's Corner House in London where my mother was employed as a waitress, or Nippy, as such angels of London refreshment houses were known. She came from a working-class district somewhere in north London, where her father had followed various occupations, including that of a police constable, and her numerous brothers were engaged in the honourable trade of plastering.

Immediately after my adoption I was whisked off by my new parents on a world-wide peregrination which only ended for me when I eventually went away to school, and for my father when he died. This happened in 1946, while I was at sea, and even then he was in the middle of selling the house and moving.

My mother was an excellent mimic and possessed an irreverent sense of Cockney humour which made her excellent company. Following her entry in my father's milieu, she soon picked up the social tricks and accents of the sort of people she encountered on board ship, or in hotels, and most of all in those palaces of snobbery, the clubs in northern India. She could switch her accent on and off like a tap, and when she wanted to irritate my father, would revert to an exaggerated form of the dialect and intonation of Seven Dials, which never failed to infuriate him.

It must have run in her family for her sister Lillian's career followed exactly the same pattern. The details are suspect, but according to my father, Lillian was scrubbing the steps of a London hospital when she caught the eye of a young doctor on his way to the wards. The effect must have been as instantaneous as my father's encounter at the Lyon's Corner House, for a speedy romance and marriage soon followed. In due course he became the Chief Medical Officer of a major British Colony in East Africa, thus enabling her to became a fully paid up member of the British Colonial Establishment. I did not meet her until after my father died, by which time her husband had retired to a hobby farm in North Devon. I withhold his name to avoid embarrassing my three cousins by adoption, though this is all so long ago it scarcely matters.

The more I think of my father the more I respect his memory. He particularly disliked career politicians and lumped them together with Socialists, Professors of Economics, teetotallers, Communists, and all foreigners with the exception of the Americans, Germans, and Scandinavians. I don't think he knew any Australians or Canadians, but they were quite acceptable, unlike the French. His special aversion were advertising men, to whom he liked to apply George Orwell's description: 'rattlers of sticks in buckets of pig-swill'. He believed that standards dropped as soon as one crossed the English Channel, and with what incandescent language would he have described the pantomime and ventriloquist's dummies in what today purports to be the 'Mother of Parliaments'!

But at least he was spared the sad spectacle of our present drug-ridden society with its pseudo-egalitarianism, mediocrity, race-riots, and street crime. If he was wrong in some things, how right he was in others. And he remains vividly in my memory, his plus-fours stuffed with cigars smuggled in from France, and always with a walking stick – not to lean on, but to flourish defiantly at the world.

At the same time I think of his India, with large cool houses, big gardens, rudimentary plumbing, and lizards glittering jewel-like on the walls. There were broad shady verandahs with long cane-chairs, and bearers hovering with trays of cool drinks, and flowering plants in terra-cotta pots – all vanished like a dream now that the long British Colonial party is over:

> Our revels now are ended. These our actors . . .
> Are melted into air, thin air,
> like this insubstantial pageant faded,
> Leave not a rack behind.

There is one recollection of my father which I include more as a period piece than anything else, for the memory of it still arouses phobias that I hope have long since been exorcised. I am not certain, but I believe the scene was Simpson's on The Strand, which thirty years later was a favourite haunt of mine when I wined and dined people during that period I have christened in this book as the 'Brief-Case Years'. It was famous for its roast joints, carved at the table, and the two house specialities: a combination of beers known as a 'Harley Street' and a 'Wimpole Street'. Its geography seemed to ring a bell when I went there in later years.

I was lunching there with my father and mother, prior to a visit to the London Zoo, when my mother, who hated seeing animals in captivity, announced that she didn't want to go, and in her penetrating voice added that it was hardly necessary anyway, since we were already apparently in one! People at nearby tables overheard this, and I cringed with embarrassment. The waiter, who was in the act of placing a bowl of soup in front of my father, muttered something under his breath, and either accidentally or deliberately put it down with a jerk that caused it to splash over my father's waistcoat. Convinced that it had been deliberate, and irritated by my mother's intransigence, my father rose from the table and grabbed the man by the collar, whereupon a majestic head waiter swam across the room accompanied by a posse of waiters, who surrounded the struggling pair. My mother, with magnificent presence of mind, calmly rose from her chair and after informing my father we would see him at home, left the room with her head held high, with me following at her heels, wishing the earth would swallow us up.

Years later, when I was home on leave during the war, I asked my father what the outcome had been. He laughed and tilted back his glass (we were in a pub at the time) and said: 'I got off with a warning. They called a policeman and I had to appear before a magistrate the next day.'

'You mean to say that you weren't even fined?' I asked incredulously. Father grinned. 'I explained that I did not assault the waiter; he assaulted me by deliberately tipping soup over me. I was merely chastising the man slightly for insolence.' I suppose in 1933 things were like that. The magistrate might even have been a retired Indian Civil Servant like himself.

When he died in 1946 my father left his estate in the form of a trust, to which my mother, to her extreme annoyance, was only entitled to the interest during her lifetime, coupled with permission to sell the current house and buy another of her choosing. My father knew what he was doing, for my mother's hobby after his death was buying and selling houses, mostly picturesque but crumbling mud cottages in Devon, and always at a loss. I had to keep signing my agreement to these transactions. I suppose she had contracted the fatal itchiness from him.

But the first house she purchased after his death did not fall into this category. She had decided to move to Cornwall, because her happiest memories were always of the west country and she chose St Austell as the base for her house-hunting activities, because it was near Mevagissy. On the first night in St Austell, she met a local man who was playing a piano in a public house, surrounded by his friends, all having a jolly sing-song. The pianist, who was in his sixties, was a bachelor and, as I discovered later, something of a local Lothario.

My mother got into a conversation with him, mentioning that she was a widow looking for a house in the area, and behold, he had a house to sell – his own, which in the event she purchased. It was a large house, with a barn and extensive buildings, from which his father had conducted an animal feed business. It was situated in the hellish village of Bugle, a straggle of grey granite houses along the main road between Bodmin and St Austell famed for its annual band-contest, and situated amid a sort of white lunar landscape of artificial hills generated by the local clay industry. My mother had to arrange for the purchase money to be paid in cash, for the vendor, Preston Thomas, did not believe in banks, and this included the inflated cost of a miscellaneous collection of ceramic bric-a-brac, which he said was of immense value. Preston came with the house, and he and my mother lived in sin for several happy years. Eventually, they married – apparently, Preston had been entangled in some extraordinary engagement which had lasted for over twenty years without getting anywhere near the altar. But when the lady died, incidentally leaving him several cottages, the happy event could go ahead. My mother and Preston were blissfully happy together, and during the summer used to motor all over Cornwall in his 1933 Austin Seven for picnics on the beach. The sequel to this affair was as hilarious as its beginning, for sadly a few years later Preston was rushed into hospital with some kind of stomach trouble and died a few days later. But on my mother's last visit to the hospital, Preston whispered in her ear that all the money she had paid for the house, plus a great deal more, was tucked away under the thick carpet which covered the stairs and landing.

I was very fond of Preston, who seemed to have left no other relatives, and I still have among my papers his photograph and family memorabilia, including a picture of him standing beside the lorry he drove in France during the First World War, which I found among my mother's effects when she died.

19

Chapter 2

MARIONETTE AND PAINTED CARTS

A childhood in the land of the Godfathers

I HAVE ALREADY MENTIONED that my father lost half his capital when England went off the gold standard, and it was then, while we were living in Pentewan, that a letter arrived from a Dr Romano, whom my father had known in northern India. Quite how a Sicilian doctor had come to set up a practice in Darjeeling in the 1920s, I do not know, unless he had twitched the toga of a Mafia godfather and had to flee the land of spaghetti, artichokes, and bilious ice-cream to escape assassination. But whatever the reason, by 1933 he had returned to his native haunts and set up a practice in Palermo from where he wrote to my father describing the delights of the island, and above all the low cost of living.

That was quite enough for father, who having lived in England for nearly a year, was probably getting itchy feet again anyway. Ignoring the fact that none of us could speak a word of Italian, within a week he had moved us into a hotel in Southampton, where he booked a passage to Naples on the Orient liner *Orama*.

I remember the shipping agent took us down to view the ship at anchor – things were done like that then – and being bitterly disappointed that it only had two funnels, and not three. It was my first real introduction to the sea, which from that day took a hold on me that has never been relinquished.

Seventy years later, I can still smell the salt-laden winds, and feel the throb of the engines and the steady vibration of that old ship at sea. And if such things are possible, she will sail forever, encapsulated in a child's memory. I still possess a small enamelled brooch in the form of a ship's steering wheel with the name 'Orama' on it in gold letters against a blue background, that my father bought for my mother in the ship's shop. And by the mysterious agency of synchronicity, which I have come to accept but cannot explain, while working this chapter, I came across a picture of the *Orama* as I was researching for another book. It shows her, bows pointing almost vertically upwards, moments before taking her last plunge, having been torpedoed during the Second World War.

At Naples we transhipped for Palermo, our mountain of luggage loaded on to several ancient gharries trailing behind a leading one containing my parents and I. As usual, I was in a state of mingled embarrassment and semi-terror – this time because my mother was complaining loudly over my father's insistence on choosing moth-eaten horses instead of motor-vehicles, and accusing him of humiliating us in order to save money. To my infant mind, the entire waterside population of Naples was laughing at the sight of our caravanserai.

Perhaps, to steal the words of Lytton Strachey, I may use the wings of historical imagination to hover briefly over the beginnings of Sicilian social history, which are buried in classical literature. The first discernable invaders were the Greeks, followed by Phoenicians, Romans and Byzantines. In the 11th century the Normans imposed their iron rule on the island, but over a period were succeeded by the Lombards. By the 14th century the Sicilians achieved independence under their own kings, and splintered into two kingdoms, each with its own king, giving rise to a succession of little civil wars. Next in the island's chequered history, it was annexed by Napoleon, and then captured by the British. In the power share-out following the defeat of the stern little Corsican megalomaniac, Austria acquired the Kingdom of Naples, which then included Sicily

The Austrians, who in their day were as despotic as Hitler, inflicted a terrible tyranny on the Italians, who could not without the greatest difficulty obtain a passport or leave the country. Discussion of politics was strictly forbidden, under pain, male or female, of being sentenced to the galleys, and foreign newspapers were banned. In Sicily this deplorable state of affairs came to an end with the liberation of Palermo by Garibaldi in 1860. By 1933, Sicily, along with the rest of Italy, was firmly under the heel of Mussolini, unkindly remembered these days as the fat bull-frog of the Pontine Marshes, even though he did make the trains run on time and kitted up a reluctant nation with weapons, black shirts and dreams of empire.

But of all this my father was as ignorant as a swan, while my mother associated Italians with ice-cream cornets and the organ grinders, complete with monkey in a small fez, who had enlivened her native haunts along the Mile-End Road.

Dr Romano met us on arrival in Palermo and we drove straight to an apartment he had arranged for us in the centre of the town. It consisted of a series of large gloomy chambers filled with heavy dark furniture, with depressing religious pictures on almost every wall. It was on the second floor of the building, with a balcony overlooking a busy street below. In hindsight it was rather like a setting from one of the early Maigret films, and just the place for a murder.

Our domestic staff consisted of an elderly female, who always wore black, with warts on her face and a moustache, who seemed to me to have stepped straight out of Grimm's *Fairy Tales*. The greasy, garlic-ridden food which appeared on our table filled us with horror, and on the second day my mother took over the cooking, which was done on a smoky oil stove. The domestic problems was compounded by the language barrier which existed between Maria and my mother – they had taken a dislike to each other on sight – but as she came with the apartment there was nothing my father could do about it. It was the custom in Palermo for people who lived in upper floor apartments like ours to conduct a large part of their shopping by lowering baskets from their balconies to vendors with carts in the street below. The process was invariably accompanied by much waving of hands and shouting, for Italians are not fitted with volume controls. This, combined with the usual street noises, created a permanent background racket, except during the afternoons, when silence descended as everyone rested up during their siesta for the next session.

Although my mother, with the aid of a dictionary, had made a list of the main items she needed to purchase, her pronunciation rendered them largely unintelligible, and she could not understand what the vendors were shouting back. It meant that transactions had to be conducted by sign language and when the question of price was reached the situation became frantic.

Among the toys which accompanied us on our travels my favourites were several regiments of lead soldiers and their artillery, which included spring-loaded field guns that could project broken matchsticks very satisfactorily halfway across the room. One evening, as Maria was departing, her exit through the door was accompanied by the sound of things falling on the floor, and a whole detachment of Gordon Highlanders together with a Maxim gun cascaded down when the elastic on her bloomers gave way under the strain of holding her booty up. My parents thought this so funny that she was forgiven, and she stayed with us until we left Palermo.

My father's daily practice was to take himself off for a walk in the mornings, which always included a visit to a bar. He would then return for a late lunch and a siesta. Afternoon tea was followed by another walk, this time accompanied by my mother and I. There was always lots to see in Palermo, and I have vivid memories of the Carretti, those splendidly decorated carts drawn by horses or mules draped in tassels and often wearing hats with holes cut in the brim to accommodate their ears. There were visits to the botanic gardens, and above all the harbour, filled with all kinds of craft, painted in brilliant colours, and all the paraphernalia of fishing – nets hanging up to dry or being mended, and fascinating green spherical glass floats.

My special favourites were the marionette and puppet shows for which Sicily is famous. Those wonderful knights in medieval armour, with huge painted eyebrows and ferocious moustaches were forever engaged in battles with lances, swords and daggers against brilliantly painted back-drops. Grand ladies with intricate hairdos and wearing elaborate dresses of velvet and lace egged them on, and the dialogue provided by the puppeteers combined with the shouts of appreciation from the crowd. Sixty-nine years later I can still remember Palermo as clearly as if it were yesterday, and, as in India, my childhood memories are filled with the clip-clopping of trotting horses, and the wholesome smell of fresh horse-dung.

As I write I have before me a picture taken of my father and myself against a background of sub-tropical plants, with a fountain playing in the background, probably in the Botanic Garden. My father is holding his Homburg hat at his side, looking rather like the 'Man Who Broke the Bank at Monte Carlo', while I am wearing a shapeless garment that comes down below my knees. I do not know whether my mother deliberately chose to inflict an androgynous appearance on me, or if it was her idea of suitable attire, but whatever the reason, she seemed to have passion for dressing me in floppy hats and button shoes, in the style of Mabel Lucie Attwell.

Among my father's old coloured postcards is one of Catania, the little town that lies at the foot of Mount Etna, the largest volcano in Europe. Actually, it is a cluster of smaller volcanoes around one large cone, and from time to time there are still explosions and molten lava flows out. The town has a Phoenix-like quality, because it has been destroyed several times over the centuries, and as if that were not enough, between eruptions the population has been decimated by the plague or cholera.

Of course my father, in spite of my mother's protestations, insisted on going up. Her fears infected me, and I had to be more or less dragged up, petrified, while they quarrelled all the way.

We were not in any danger, because we were part of a party conducted by a guide, but I clearly remember the alarming approach to the crater viewpoint, across a stretch of grey dried lava, and the sight of the cone itself emitting clouds of sulphurous steam. It was not at all pleasant, and as we walked we left footprints in the lava, which emitted little puffs of steam.

It could not have been long before we returned to England. My father must have seen the political writing on the wall as Mussolini's 'Black-Shirts' intruded ever more into ordinary life. I remember that even in easy-going Palermo there were, every day, black-shirted children marching along, shouting in unison: 'Una Dua, Una Dua', in imitation of Hitler's Youth.

On our return to England my father rented a house on the front in Brighton, and where my mother, during an argument with him, hurled a stuffed crocodile down the front steps on to the pavement below. But that is another story, which I shall spare the reader.

Chapter 3

MY INDIA

> For the temple bells are calling,
> And it's there that I would be,
> By the old Moulmein Pagoda,
> Lookin' lazy at the sea.
>
> *Rudyard Kipling*

THE PLACE WHERE YOU spend your childhood lays its hand upon you, and that is what India has done to me, as it has to every other child brought in the old British Raj. And mine was perhaps the last generation to truly have had this experience, before British rule – then at its last gasp – finally disappeared.

In my mind, India, Pakistan and Burma are not partitioned; they remain as part of a whole, itself but a passing chapter in the long history of the sub-continent. Only now do I understand how transitory and what a mixed bag of achievement and failure the British Raj was, and how scandalous was the manner of our handing it back. On the plus side were the roads, the railways, the dams and canals, and the dedicated work done by individual District Officers to administer justice to the Indians under their care, as fairly as a bureaucracy-ridden administration allowed them.

Set against that must be the appalling snobbery which excluded Indians socially. Even a Maharajah educated at Eton or Oxford, and on personal terms with King George V, was not welcome at the Bombay Yacht Club. The poor of India, who constitute the majority of the population, ask nothing more than to pray to whatever God they worship to grant them security of life and property, and to enjoy the fruits of their labours And for so many, even today, now that India has achieved independence, it is a prayer that is never answered.

But in deploring the manner in which we handed it back, equally I reject the blame popularly heaped on Lord Louis Mountbatten, the last Viceroy of India, for 'rushing through' partition, and 'not ensuring that the British army prevented the Hindus, Muslims and Sikhs from looting and massacring each other'. Lord Louis was handed this problem by a socialist government only concerned to rid itself of India as soon as possible, regardless that India was being divided into inherently unstable units, which were social, economic and religious disasters waiting to happen. At the root of it all lay the fundamental religious hatreds and jealousies of the Indian people themselves, refined in the persons of Ghandi, Nehru, and Jinnah. Given the situation with which he was confronted, it was beyond the power of Mountbatten or anyone else to contain it with the forces at his disposal. He recognised this, and to act with commendable speed was about all that was left to him.

India had always been a chaotic land characterised by incessant civil wars, steeped in corruption, where the rich trampled on the poor. The heavy hand of the Moguls had produced a limited semblance of law and order and given India its magnificent heritage of Mogul buildings and gardens. Then came the British, imposing their own ideas, and eventually establishing a modern infra-structure and commercial empire. Handing it back has merely led to a westernised version of the old order where the Nawabs and Maharajahs have been replaced by politicians and industrialists. The Princes at least possessed eccentric charm and provided a spectacle for the people, and an exotic background for their excesses and exploitations.

The worst excesses occurred in the Punjab where the Sikhs were basically responsible for the wholesale nature of the massacres, for they were determined to ensure that the bulk of their community formed part of either India or Pakistan but not split up between the two.

It was only Ghandhi's extraordinary power over the masses that prevented massacres on a similar scale in Bengal, and his tragedy was that while his dream had been for a united independent India, it was he who in the end was chiefly responsible for partition. Ghandhi above all else was driven by his Hinduism. It was he who finally convinced Jinnah that the Hindus would never allow the Muslims an equal voice in Congress, and thus destroyed any hope of a Muslim/Hindu coalition. And in the end he was assassinated by one of his own followers. It was aptly remarked that it cost more to transport Ghandhi about the country with his road show of spinning-wheel and penniless asceticism than if he had been a Maharajah.

Nehru, in spite of his western education and secular beliefs, was no better. For all his bright promises, he soon picked a quarrel with little Goa, and then annexed it. Then in the glow of that achievement he began a war with China, who routed his army in a few days, and could, if they had wished, taken Delhi. Instead, the Chinese, who like the Catholic Church, think in centuries ahead, turned back. Unlike Nehru, they were not interested in clouds of glory; India could wait.

By any rational divisional of India, Kashmir, with its predominantly Muslim population, should be part of Pakistan, just as Calcutta was the natural port of East Pakistan, that short-lived geographical monstrosity that only politicians could have created. Twice India, with its massive military superiority, has gone to war with Pakistan, and would clearly like to overwhelm it, and as I write these words they are on the brink of war again. But nuclear weapons even up the odds, and the future remains to be seen. It is only the poor of India, Pakistan, and Kashmir, already stripped of most of the rewards of their labours by politicians, who have, as usual, to pay the price.

A child, especially a young child, is close to the ground, from which all life springs, and is more aware of the fragrant earthy smells of green vegetation and the little creatures that live amongst it. Thus, it is for me that my earliest memories are tied up with the dusk and dawn chorus of frogs croaking, the mingled scents of an Indian garden, the clip-clop of a trotting Tonga pony's hooves, and the wholesome smell of fresh dung on a dusty sun-drenched road. I am comfortingly aware of the bright colours of my Ayah's shawl and sari, and the sun glinting on the gold ring through her nose, and her silver bangles, and her reassuring presence. She is crooning some Indian nursery rhyme, and I can still remember some of the words: 'Nini Kurro, Butcha' – 'Go to sleep, little one'.

The children of the Raj were utterly spoiled by servants, and grew up believing that India belonged to them, which in a way it did. It was not until I returned to England that this, the first of many illusions, was shattered. I like best the story of one such infant, who soon after landing, enquired of its parents: 'Why are all the natives white?' Even better, was the specially privileged child who wanted to know: 'Why the train had left the station without the station-master asking Daddy's permission?'

Gardens were always lawns fringed with terra-cotta pots filled with flowers, usually geraniums, and in one corner there would be a cement tank filled with dark green water and myriads of tiny wriggling things. Ours, my father assured me, was the home of a crocodile that emerged after dark in search of tasty morsels, and particularly liked succulent little children who ought to have been in bed.

He would lift me on his shoulder, and give me a piece of sugar cane to suck. And I can never forget, when I graduated from floppy hats, the distinctive cork smell of the cool green interior of my own miniature white sola topi. Then there was the morning when I saw the snake. There it was, sinister and menacing, with a black ribbed skin, coiled in a perfect circle in the middle of the lawn. My shrieks summoned the Himal – the gardener – who vanished like a streak of lightning in search of our Chowkidar – the watchman – who was always armed with a long brass-bound stick called a lathi. The snake remained perfectly still, and circling it with commendable caution, he gradually got near enough to deal it a crashing blow with his lathi. It did not appear to move, so he hit it again and again. By this time my mother had arrived, just in time to witness the anticlimax – it was an old bicycle-tyre!

When I was nearly seven I contracted colitis, and according to my mother my life was saved by the Sicilian doctor Romano. What he was doing in Darjeeling in 1932 I do not know, but on his advice my parents brought me back to England, where my father alighted briefly in Brighton in a rented house overlooking the sea. In the hall there was a suit of armour which kept falling over, and a stuffed crocodile, which my father had carefully dragged near the door to frighten calling tradesmen. Another feature was a huge cast iron hall-stand covered with vines and flowers made of metal, which my father assured me was the home of a family of poisonous snakes. Every time we went out I had to be dragged past it, screaming. I don't think he was being deliberately cruel, he just had a peculiar sense of humour.

I did not visit the sub-continent again until 1944, when I was the Chief Radio Officer of an American-built 'Liberty' ship named the *Samdel*, which carried war supplies to Rangoon, then not long liberated from the Japanese. It gave me the opportunity to look for the house my father had when he was Deputy Collector in Rangoon before the First World War, though all I had to go on was the photograph which appears in the illustrations. But I did locate it undamaged but distressed and transmogrified into a rabbit-warren occupied by Burmese and Anglo-Burmese families. An old friend of mine, a Burmese who has now settled in England and visits Rangoon regularly, tells me it has long since been pulled down, along with its neighbours, to make way for modern development.

My father owned property in Rangoon, as well as in India, which still belonged to him after his early retirement from the Indian Civil Service in 1921. I remember that all through my childhood a monthly letter would arrive from a firm of lawyers in Rangoon called Balthazar & Son who looked after his investments there. When he died in 1946 they passed to me as part of the trust he set up in his will. Of course they had yielded no interest during the war years, and the whole lot vanished with

Burmese independence. In later years, when the Marconi Wireless Telegraph Company were setting up land links in Burma, and consequently had money transactions with the Burmese government, I tried without success to get some funds back in a legal manner, taking advantage of the situation, but not surprisingly it was hopeless.

Like everybody else who goes to Rangoon I visited the Shwe Dagon Pagoda, reputedly the largest in the world and once crowned with gold leaf. Because of my distaste for travelogues I spare the reader yet one more description, but I cannot pass the horror with which I viewed it without comment. The place was filthy dirty and littered with pi-dogs, those unfortunate, starving, neglected strays one sees all over the East. They were in various stages of emaciation and being literally devoured by flies. There were cats as well, vainly trying to lick themselves clean in the way that cats do. Extreme cruelty to animals seems to be a characteristic of the Buddhist countries I have visited. Their religion forbids them to take life, even by swallowing a gnat, but apparently says nothing about preserving it; that responsibility belongs to fate, and is not their business. It is something I always think about when I am accosted in London by young men and women prancing about in orange robes and saluting me with 'Hare Krishna!' and a silly grin.

It is the same with the endless prayers, lighting candles, and ringing bells. Ringing a bell counts as a prayer, and one can pass along a line of bells hanging on a monastery wall, tapping each one as you go along, and build up a substantial credit balance with very little effort. Prayer wheels, engraved with suitable texts, are even better; you just spin them and bathe in the ineffable glow that follows. I am told they even have them connected to water-wheels in private gardens, so that that the householder is bathed in a perpetual mist of religious devotion.

From Rangoon we went up the Hooghly to Calcutta, where the Indians were busy demonstrating their feelings towards the British Raj by feeding European executives of the Tata Steelworks into the furnaces! We lay alongside at Kiddapore Docks for three weeks while we loaded a full cargo of coal destined for the blast furnaces at Immingham (Ming-Ming, as we used to call it). There were no coal-tips; instead human conveyor belts in the form of Indian women with baskets on their heads walked up wooden ramps from the quayside, two to each hold, and emptied their baskets over the edge. The process continued day and night until loading was completed.

Calcutta at that time had a distinct flavour of an Errol Flynn Hollywood war movie, for it was heaving with troops, British and American, who filled night-spots like Firpo's, Greens, and the Winter Gardens, to capacity. Stamped in my memory are the Sikh taxi-drivers, Jehus who drove their pre-war American Fords with flapping khaki canvas hoods with total indifference to any other user of the road, machine, man, or animal.

But I had a family chore to carry out in Calcutta. During the eighteen seventies and eighties, my adoptive grandfather had conducted a fashionable medical practice there which my father claimed had even included members of the Vice-Regal circle. I knew that the house and surgery had been in Free School Street, for among my father's photographs were several old sepia prints mounted on crumbling yellow cardboard showing what presumably was my grandfather's gharry and uniformed driver in the street outside a large walled compound. I located Free School Street without much difficulty, and it proved as much a disappointment as the historic Chandni Chowk in Old Delhi when I visited that in later years. At one time it had been an elegant street lined with the houses of Europeans, each in their own grounds, with rows of stables, outbuildings, and servants' quarters. Things had sadly changed; the spaces between the houses had been filled up with jerry-built crumbling shop-fronts with rickety balconies and peeling masonry stained with betel juice. At one time the road must have had a sort of miniature canal running along one side; no doubt in my grandfather's day it had been clear water. Now it was a choked open sewer reeking of ammonia fumes and the smell of excreta, human and animal. It was filled with a perpetual traffic jam of cycle-rickshaws, jostling pedestrians, hand carts and cows feeding from the stalls of vegetable-vendors, while cars, blowing their horns continuously, slowly wormed their way through the tangled mass of activity.

In India the cow is sacred, and its urine is regarded both as a universal medicine and a wholesome drink, as was publicly demonstrated by Mr Desai, who succeeded Nehru as Prime Minister. This gentleman drank a glassful of cow's urine every morning, which made him rather unpleasant to sit next to in hot weather, but his Hinduism was acclaimed by the masses, in contrast to his secular and secretly humanist predecessor. Cow's dung is carefully collected and hand-patted into small bricks which make excellent cooking fuel, and has a hundred other uses, with the result that in India the soil is never enriched by natural compost, apart from human, which is everywhere. And being sacred, a cow is permitted to browse wherever it can find a tasty morsel, in practice usually from vendors' stalls. They lie down in the streets, where the cars have to go around them, and a cow must never be killed, though there is no rule that it must be fed, which is why India is filled with emaciated cows who give very little milk.

In 1952 I found myself again in India, or rather Pakistan, as that part of it had then become, sent there by the Marconi Marine Company as Assistant to the Manager. There were local technicians, but in fact mine was a hands-on job, for we serviced every kind of electronic equipment on shipboard – communication, navigational, and radar, of any manufacture and on any nationality of ship.

The manager, Thomas Moriarty, was from Dingle in the west coast of Ireland, and as Irish as the shamrock and poteen, with a gift of language that would charm a bird off a tree. After eighteen months he returned to the UK and I found myself in the position of acting Depot Manager; what might be called meteoric promotion.

The port of Karachi, situated on the edge of the Sind Desert, where it only rains about twice a year, was in 1952 a delightful place to spend three years of one's early career. The horrors of partition had faded, leaving several gigantic refugee camps which had arisen to house the millions of Muslims fleeing from massacre in Delhi and the Punjab. The British clubs and banks, insurance companies and shipping agents were still operating very much as before. People dressed in the evenings to go to the clubs, and though Pakistanis were not officially excluded, very few were to be seen. A few very wealthy Pakistani families, including Parsee shipowners, were members but they rarely made an appearance. Probably they had better things to do, and more desirable company to keep.

The majority of the members were, like myself, engaged in commercial activities, and it seemed to be the wives who mostly kept up the colour bar, shuddering with horror at the thought of associating with Pakistanis using the club. How pathetic it all was; translated typists and shop-assistants attempting an Eliza Dolittle. The old colonial clockwork, though it would never be re-wound, had still a little time to run. The Muslim country of Pakistan during those years was friendly, religiously tolerant, and full of hopes for the future, sadly never to be fulfilled.

The people in India whose friendship I cherish most are Sikhs, Parsees, and Brahims; those salt of Indian earth. In Karachi my work brought me into close contact with the Parsee family of Cowasjee, the major ship-owners of the new country. Parsees are basically Persians, believers in the ancient religion of Zoraster, who emigrated to India around the 10th century to escape Muslim persecution, and still preserve their faith in all its purity.

Of all the faiths in the world, Zorasterism appeals to me the most. Its adherents revere fire, not in superstitious worship, but as a symbol of their belief in the indestructibility of the human soul. Just as a series of small fires, if brought together, will merge into a single larger one, so the Parsees believe that human souls merge after death and return to that mysterious starting point from whence they came.

Fire reduces all things to their beginnings; it is the great purifier, and when Parsees die in India, their bodies are placed on an iron grid at the top of one of their towers of silence where their bones are picked clean by the birds of the air and eventually drop through the bar as dust to the kindly earth below. What more satisfactory way could there be in a hot country to dispose of the bodies of the dead?

Not very long after Tom Moriarty went back to the UK, a Norwegian cargo ship named the *Toledo* went ashore off Karachi. The Cowasjees, entrepreneurs that they were, decided to enter the salvage business, acquiring an ex-Admiralty tug, the *Salvigil*, for the purpose. The firm's office was in an Edwardian building in Keamari, at the far end of the Karachi docks, aptly named 'Buckingham Palace Mansions', for it was a miniature replica of the royal dwelling in London, so christened and built by the Cowasjee of the day in honour of the King-Emperor. Rustam Cowasjee, the then head of the family, did not himself operate from there but from his large private house in Clifton, the residential area of Karachi. It was decided that I should install a radio-telephone transceiver on the bridge of the *Toledo* – in 1954 mobile phones had not been invented – and a corresponding one in his house, so that Rustam could personally keep up-to-date with how operations were proceeding. After what, to put it mildly, was a hair-raising passage out to the *Toledo* in a motor launch in monsoon seas, I installed the equipment, and for several months thereafter I found myself summoned to the house at all hours of the day and night, because the equipment had become the family's favourite toy, and simple though it was, they always seemed to have difficulty in operating it.

One weekend I was summoned at about nine o'clock in the evening, and shown, very informally attired, into the huge drawing room which served as the nerve centre of Rustam's massive business empire, which was not confined to ships and Karachi. It seemed to be conducted from the largest dining room table that I had ever seen in my life, which was heaped with folders, piles of correspondence, copies of *Lloyd's List*, and recent issues of the *Financial Times*. It was a fascinating insight into how a multi-millionaire Parsee businessman operated an international business under the nose of an inquisitive government, which had not yet quite got around to ensuring that avoidance of its currency regulations was restricted to its own members.

The room was full of Cowasjees, including Rustam himself, and as I entered they all burst into roars of laughter. I felt like a character in a Bateman cartoon and struggled to conceal my irritation. It was outside normal hours; I was tired, and all my friends were relaxing at the club. But Rustam was far and away my most important customer, and my efforts to nail an agreeable smile on my face must have resulted in a horrible grimace. Then one of the daughters – they were all products of an English boarding school education – grinned and explained what they had all found so funny.

It seemed that just before my arrival Rustam had been severely lecturing the younger members of his family on the dangers of having been born with golden spoons in their mouths, and holding me up as a glowing example of the virtues of hard work and early responsibility.

I have never forgotten Rustam Cowasjee, and I salute his memory. The Cowasjees and the other great Parsee families of Bombay and Calcutta had been established as far afield as Aden and Port Said since the days of sailing ships. They began as ship's chandlers, but it was not long before they added ship-owning and building to their businesses. And the names of the great Parsee commercial families of India, like Mr Soda-Water Wallah, and Jee-Jee Boy, indicated the humble beginnings from which their great enterprises had sprung.

There was Jehanghir Ratanji Dadabhoy Tata, the first Indian to obtain an A flying licence, and who founded what later became Air India. And in Calcutta had been his mentor, Sir Dorab Tata, Chairman of Tata, whose steelworks provided the material for the manufacture of steam-engines, railway lines, and lorries, and virtually created industrial India. Dadabhoy Tata was a truly international character, who now lies buried in the family mausoleum at Pierre Lachaise in Paris, in accordance with his wishes.

Parsees usually marry within their community, though sometimes an exception is made, because they like to preserve the strain of fairer skins of their Persian forebears. I had the great privilege of being invited to the wedding of Ardeshir Cowasjee, a powerfully built young man with a pointed thick black beard, whom I always thought should have been mounted on a war-horse and wearing a steel corslet and helmet, and slashing down his foes, rather than working in the family business in Karachi. It was a fairy tale affair, which went on all day and into the evening amid gardens hung with coloured lights and tables groaning under sumptuous repasts.

How safe and happy and secure, and full of hope for the future was Karachi in the early 1950s, before political corruption engulfed the state, followed by the gun-and-moustache men, and finally the mad fundamentalism of the mullahs. It was safe to walk anywhere, including the crowded refugee camps. In the evenings especially, the bazaars, their stalls piled high with goods of every description, but particularly cloths and silks, became a vast open-air Aladdin's Cave, filled with amiable gossiping sight-seeing shoppers, and with everywhere the delicious smells of spicy Indian cuisine being cooked on street-side braziers. Crazy electric lighting, strung between anywhere that would support the cables, was supplemented by pump-up Aladdin lamps, and the smoky flickering glow of oil lamps made from a Barclays beer can filled with oil with a wick stuck in the top. The soft evening air was filled with the haunting strains of Indian music, and the women in their brilliant saris created a riot of colour, drifting past with the swaying grace that is the birthright of Indian women. It is a memory that more than half a century later seems to be only yesterday.

In my office once a week I used to receive a visit from a Catholic priest, a giant of a man in a brown cassock, leather sandals and a khaki sola topi – a form of headgear which by then was no longer worn by Europeans. He was a visitor I inherited from my predecessor, who had always provided him with tea and a donation for his church, a practice that I continued, although then, as now, I was not a member of any organised religion. His parish consisted of the refugee camps, of whom only a tiny proportion were catholic, and he had to entirely subsist on what these desperately poor people could spare. He was always cheerful, and one week he arrived in a state not far off euphoria.

Apparently, it was a double celebration; after thirteen years in India he was half way through his tour of duty, and the previous week had seen the consecration of his church, which I promised to visit. It turned out to be a small corrugated iron shed on the edge of a vast refugee camp, and the sight of it enraged me. At Clifton, the diplomatic residential area and the most salubrious spot in Karachi, was the Vatican embassy filled with well-dressed priests who were to be seen at all the diplomatic garden parties, conveyed there in chauffeur-driven American cars. When I asked me friend about them, he smiled silently and shook his head – there was only the most tenuous of connections with the business next door.

Tolerant though Karachi was of the foreigners working in its midst, as a Muslim country pork was strictly off limits, but out at the airport at the end of the Drigh Road, Europeans could order bacon and eggs at the airport restaurant or at one of the various airline rest-houses. In those leisured and saner days, BOAC, KLM, and PAN-AM, one flew to Australia in a series of hops, and slept in a comfortable bed each night, and the airlines had their rest-houses at Karachi. Of course, it took longer, but did that really matter? One was not then ignominiously squeezed up like a sardine, and as one dear old Indian once put it to me, 'What do you do with all this time when you have saved it?'

At the end of my tour and it was time to come home the question of income tax had to be settled, for one could not leave the country without a tax clearance certificate. In those happy far-off days in Pakistan, Europeans were not troubled by income tax until they left the country, when a tax certificate was required. A few weeks before I was due to depart I went to the tax office to settle up. It was housed in a dusty fly-blown building with a row of wooden chairs for the customers. From it could be seen, in an adjoining room, the European tax filing arrangements, which consisted of piles of buff-coloured folders tied up with pink ribbon (yes, pink ribbon, the Indian babu's sacred inheritance from the Raj). Originally, the piles had each been one for a letter of the alphabet, but most had fallen sideways into each other, and it looked like a mountain of scruffy folders. The secret, I had been advised beforehand, was to 'grease' the clerk's palm on the way in, in order locate your file in the pile so that it could be dealt with.

Then in due course you went back for a friendly chat with the Tax Inspector, at the end of which he would mention the name of a nearby restaurant where you could both take tea. It was understood that before parting a process would take place which our American cousins, with their gift for financial euphemisms, term 'the accommodation'. In my case it turned out to be a highly satisfactory arrangement for both parties, and we parted vowing eternal friendship. How totally corrupt and delightful was Karachi in those far-off happy days!

But it is not of that I wish really to speak. A row of applicants was already in place when I took my seat, which was next to a very dark Anglo-Indian lady – almost black; probably part-Dravidian from the south of India. She was fat, exhausted-looking, wearing a shapeless flowery dress and worn black court shoes painfully distorted by bunions and had a plastic shopping bag at her side.

Following me was a self-important looking man who seemed to be, like Billy Bennett, not quite a gentleman, and when the clerk called for the next person to go into the tax collector's office, he leapt up, in spite of being the last in the queue. The black lady then electrified everyone, including me, by saying, in a very loud voice and in the unmistakable accent of Roedean, 'DO YOU MIND!'

The wretched queue-jumper seemed to shrivel up like a snail with salt put on it, while the owner of the voice turned to me and remarked, 'THESE BLOODY PEOPLE – WHAT A PERFORMANCE!'

It was fascinating, a remarkable example of the potency and arrogant self-confidence conferred by a top British public school education. I often wonder who she was, and how she came to be sitting in that waiting-room, and indeed what became of her. My theory is that she was a member of some princely family, sent to school in England between the wars, and displaced and impoverished by the confusion of divided India. I like to think that she went to England, where she might have had friends, and ended her days in some sort of comfort.

Finally, I returned to the UK as I went out, as a passenger in the Anchor Line *Cilicia*, and this gave me the unforgettable experience of making the journey home in the old comfortable style, where passengers dressed for dinner, and placed bets on the ship's day's run. It took three weeks, and never again would an employee of the Marconi Company or any others enjoy such a long paid break. The era of the great liners to India and the Far East had gone for ever, and the *Cilicia* and her sister ship the *Circassia* were broken up soon afterwards. How lucky I was to see its end! And how sad.

Twelve years later I again returned to India, this time as part of an extended tour of Marconi Marine's depots in the Middle East, Pakistan, India, Bangladesh, and East Africa. But I omit the travelogue, except for two incidents.

During my visit to Bombay, I gave a reception on behalf of the Marconi Marine Company at the Taj Mahal Hotel, when the guest list included nearly everybody of consequence in Indian shipping. It included the Indian Director of Shipping, Admiral Sampson of the Mazagon Dry Dock, the Captain of the training ship *Dufferin*, and the leading figures of all the local shipping companies Also on the list was the British Trade Commissioner, a fat young man, whom I later heard did a very good snake dance at parties. Surprisingly, or perhaps not so surprisingly, he astounded me by remarking that he had never heard of Marconi Marine – after all, we had only been there fifty years!

I was occupying a modest room in the Taj, but when I consulted the manager to arrange the reception, his eyes nearly popped out of his head at the sight of the guest list, for in independent India there is nothing that the chattering classes enjoy better than a cocktail party well stocked with important names. He immediately wanted to transfer me to an apartment more suited to my exalted status, but I refused, being more concerned with how one gave a successful mid-day function in a place that was 'dry', as Bombay was at the time. A European could get alcoholic drinks without breaking the law by officially registering as an alcoholic, which you automatically did when you booked into a hotel; the form was handed to you when you signed the register. But I need not have worried. The manager, with exquisite charm and a quiet smile, explained that the house had a special range of 'fruit cocktails' more than adequate to the occasion.

A superb buffet was laid and I had the never-to-be-forgotten experience of welcoming my guests and their wives; undoubtedly, the most glamourous array of female beauty one could ever wish to behold, in fantastic saris, that most charming of all feminine dress, and decked with elegant jewellery, like a gathering of exotic birds of paradise.

My other memory is of Calcutta, where our manager had booked me into the Grand Hotel. On the inside of my bedroom door was a huge deadbolt, obviously recently added. Above it was a notice in blotched red ink 'BOLT YOUR DOOR'. I mentioned this next morning when he picked me up. 'Ah!' he explained, 'a few days ago an American couple were murdered in their beds in the room next door and their money stolen.' That was thirty-four years ago. I trust things are better now, but from what I have heard I don't feel very hopeful.

Chapter 4

PALACES, FORTS, DACOITS, AND MANIC DRIVERS

A drive through India from Bombay to Kashmir

IN 1973 I RETURNED TO SEA for ten happy years, my last two voyages being spent on the *Marilock*, a large bulk carrier managed by the northeast coast firm of Turnbull-Scott. As well as two circumnavigations we were tramping in the north Pacific (that least pacific of oceans), and the Far East.

At the end of the first voyage, which lasted for over a year, I left the sea and set up a business venture in Swansea, which was doomed from the start, for it was the one thing in my life I have ever begun without being filled with enthusiasm.

It was not long before I realised that things were not going to work out, but it took me nine months to escape without losing my capital. Then, like my hero and fugleman, the explorer Sir Richard Burton, I sought to flee the country, which in my case meant a return to sea.

I telephoned the marine superintendent of Turnbull-Scott to see if they had any vacancies for radio officers, and found by another of the extraordinary workings of fate that seem to govern my life, that the *Marilock*, for the first time in years, was fixed for the UK. Not only that, she was due in Port Talbot, just down the road from Swansea where I live, in a few days time, and if I wished to replace the existing radio officer they would make the necessary arrangements.

It was an extraordinary experience to again go aboard and re-occupy the large and comfortable cabin which had already been my home for more than a year of my life.

An Indian crew came out from Bombay to join at the same time, the most senior of whom was a second mate named Mohan Chabba, and with my Indian connections we formed a warm friendship which continues to this day. Then followed nine happy months tramping across the North Atlantic and around the Mediterranean. There was a young master in command, Captain Falconer, who ran his ship with a mixture of friendliness and easy good discipline that was never abused. For me, that period was a sort of swansong for the old British Merchant Navy, never to return, and if these words ever enter the field of vision of Captain Falconer, I send him my good wishes and thanks.

Eleven years later, Mohan Chabba, by then Captain Chabba, and commanding large modern ships out of Hong Kong and being paid in American dollars, invited me to go to India and join him on a drive through India from Bombay to the Punjab, from where I could go on from his home in Amritsar to Kashmir. Mohan sailed on seven-month voyages with five months leave, and at the end of one of these I could stay with him in Lonavala, a hill station in the Western Ghats just north of Bombay, where he was building a house. I could use that as a base while I had a look around southern India, and then we would drive up to Amritsar in his air-conditioned Japanese car, visiting all points of interest on the way.

India has been much exposed to travelogues and I have tried to pick out items which might be interesting, and relate to people rather than places.

India is as vast as it is crowded; a land of contrast stretching from the Himalayas to Cape Comorin in the far south. The food ranges from magnificent to terrible, and the pollution, dirt, poverty, and corruption is almost beyond description. Tap water can be lethal, even if you just brush your teeth with it, and the same applies to salads and fruit, with the exception of bananas, which Nature has wrapped in her own dirt-proof package. It is difficult to go to India without having tummy troubles. Outside the big cities even if you stay at a modern hotel, the cook who pats up your Scotch Egg may have just used a toilet consisting of four bare concrete walls with one tap of cold water and a tin mug – and no paper.

If you walk anywhere in a city or at a place of interest and are identified as a tourist, you will be permanently surrounded by a crowd of Indians endeavouring to sell you things or services, or trying to get into a conversation leading to the same thing. You will be followed by cycle-rickshaws who pester to such an extent that you have to jump on board because it becomes impossible to walk.

But go into the villages and countryside and you will find the people of an older India, who are friendly and welcoming, and proud, and who are the salt of India's earth.

Mohan, though he is clean-shaven and does not wear a turban, is a Sikh of Sikhs, with all the toughness of his warrior ancestors, and I am not exactly an innocent. But it was not until we were well on our way that we realised the foolhardiness of what we had begun. Mohan had with him the acquisitions accumulated on his last voyage; things like expensive cameras and a modern steel cross-bow, complete with re-useable arrows, unobtainable in India But above all we had money, enough to set up an Indian village for life.

Once you leave the main roads in India and plunge into the country districts you become at risk from opportunistic thieves, and worse still, Dacoits – gangs of armed robbers who appear from nowhere and melt away again as quickly, usually merging back into the villages from where they came. The situation is aggravated by the extreme poverty of India and the absence of effective and non-corruptible policing. Probably the nearest policeman is fifty miles away, and he would run a mile in the opposite direction anyway, in the event of any trouble. That is if he were not in league with the robbers! Driving in a remote country district a traveller may come across a tree trunk placed across the road. You stop, and out step a group of armed men who point a gun at you and beckon you from your car . If you are lucky, they will take your car and drive off with it, with all your papers and possessions, instead of knocking you on the head, pushing the car into a ditch, with you in it, and setting fire to it – yet another unfortunate accident in India!

Even on the main roads of India it is common for a policeman or soldier to stop your car and ask to see your papers, or driving licence, or purport to inspect your tyres. A ten rupee note and a cigarette will quickly solve the matter, and off you go again. It is no good being annoyed; you are in India, and that is how things are done. If you cannot accept dirt, pollution, and corruption, you have no business in India, which would be a pity, because it is the most fascinating and exciting country in the world.

Even the main roads are pot-holed, and often flooded, with crumbling edges that frequently fade into steep ditches. In India only a tiny proportion of the money allocated to the infrastructure, say roads, ends up being actually spent on their maintenance; the rest goes into pockets from Ministers down to the last link in the chain, probably an untouchable who fills up the holes from a wheelbarrow and covers them with a bucket of hot tar. A few weeks later you can't see where he's been.

Even the remote villages seem to be heavily populated; people, carts, bullocks, cows and children wander under the wheels of your car. And woe betide the foreigner who runs over a pedestrian, especially a child. The chances are you would be lynched and your car set on fire.

On the main roads lorries are driven mostly by Sikh drivers who regard every other driver on the road as a direct challenge to their masculinity. Horns blowing continuously, they weave in and out of traffic in a mad dance with death. Most of the lorries are badly maintained, belching clouds of black diesel fumes, or running off the road because the steering has failed or the back axle has collapsed. It is common to be driving along on your side of the road and see a lorry heading directly at you on your side; and to avoid death you have to swerve out of the way.

Daman, Baroda, Udaipur, Chittorgagh, Kota, Agra, the ruined Mogul city of Fatehpur Sikri, the great National Park of Ram thambor, Jaipur, Delhi, Amritsar with its golden temple, Srinigar, and the Dal Lake in Kasmir – I have three Sainsbury's boxes filled with photographs awaiting the day when I get around to putting them in albums. And even then, who will want to look at them when the individual who took them, and for whom they have such meaning, has departed to the Happy Hunting Grounds?

Among the most impressive sights in India must be the hilltop forts, now mostly deserted ruins, which seem to encapsulate the romantic heroism of the besiegers and besieged and the colourful drama of India's past history. They sprawl along hilltops overlooking a plain or a valley, their arresting silhouette overwhelmingly dramatic, especially if you catch them at dawn or as night is falling. I have seen many in India, but the fortress of Chittorgagh in Rajastan is the one I remember most. It sums up the whole romantic ideal of Rajput chivalry; three times in its history it was sacked amid scenes of unbelievable ferocity. The first was when Ala-ud-din-Khilji, the Pathan king of Delhi, took it in 1303 to capture the beautiful Padmini, married to the uncle of the ruler. The end came when, hopelessly outnumbered, the men rode out of the fort to certain death, while the women built a huge funeral pyre and threw themselves upon it.

The same thing happened again in 1535, when the Sultan of Gujurat besieged the fort, and then in 1568 in the final sack of Chittorgagh history repeated itself when Akbar stormed the fort. The ruler, Udai Singh, fled to Udaipur where he established a new capital. In 1616 Jehangir returned Chittorgagh to the Rajputs, but they did not move back.

The other feature of India is the temples, of which I have seen so many that I cannot remember their names. But they all have a common characteristic; each one appears to be in the hands of a particular family, who hand it down from generation to generation as in the UK one might inherit a family business. The faithful come from far and wide, to temples like the sacred shrines of Kedernath and Badrinath in the foothills of the Himalayas, where pilgrims might have travelled even from the south of India.

The offerings of the faithful go directly into the pockets of the family who control the shrine; a never-ending source of tax-free income.

One particular temple I visited was situated on top of a high hill, and approached by a series of steps winding their way up to the temple. The approach, including the steps, was lined with stalls selling refreshments and souvenirs, and from them the pilgrims could purchase the offering they made to the temple god, which invariably took the form of vegetables and always a coconut. Having purchased, from their scanty means, their offering, the pilgrims would deposit them at the shrine. There, at a convenient time, they would be removed by the temple guardians, and returned to the stalls to be sold again. The coconuts, being almost indestructible, could be re-cycled almost indefinitely. As Mr Arthur Daly would put it, 'A nice little earner!'

But strangely enough I do not regard the temple guardians with the same distaste I do Indian politicians, who nowadays are often ex-criminals and masters of corruption. Even more distressing are the beggars and lepers, and children mutilated at birth who hold out their hands for alms. It is not good to incur the curses of such as they; better to make a small offering and pass on one's way.

At Amritsar I stayed with Mohan at his family home for a week, and visited the fabulous Golden Temple, holy place of the Sikhs, and the Jallianwala Bagh where on 13th April, 1919, General Dyer ordered his troops to fire on a defenceless crowd of peaceful demonstrators, producing 1,516 casualties in fifteen minutes. What is there to say, except to express amazement that on his return to the UK this murderer was presented with a large sum of money by those who thought 'he had saved India for the British'.

I was determined to go up to Kashmir, in spite of the warnings of all my friends. The place, with its legendary Dal Lake and house-boats, had captured my imagination ever since my childhood, and I still have a faded photograph of the great peak of Nanga Parbat from Gulmarg taken with my mother's Box Brownie.

My first and only encouragement came when I booked my flight to Srinigar at the Air India office in Amritsar. 'I suppose you think I'm silly to go there,' I remarked to the Sikh gentleman who wrote out my ticket. He smiled, and shook his head. 'If you go with a good heart, no harm will come to you.' I found his words curiously comforting, and they have sustained me on other occasions since then.

The plane was full, but only three were other tourists; an English girl in a poncho, hippyish and confident in an upper class sort of way, and a westernised Indian couple who were to naturalised Canadians whose family had been turned out of Uganda by Idi Amin.

Aluddin and Shaila had been given good advice by friends in Delhi about the situation in Srinigar, and were kind enough to share it with me. Apparently, the trick was to keep clear of Srinigar town, which was extremely dangerous, and on arrival at the airport take a taxi, driven by a Pathan driver, to the lake. There you took a 'shikar', a sort of small boat paddled from the stern and went directly to the houseboats. Aluddin and Shaila had been given an introduction to the Kashmiri gentleman who owned a string of the most desirable ones, and there they were, tied up in a row, all empty.

The quarrel between India and Pakistan over Kashmir, which had simmered ever since the partition of India, had boiled over on both sides. That was in 1995, as I write these words in 2002 the two countries are on the verge of war, restrained only by the horrific possibilities of nuclear weapons. By any rational division Kashmir, with it's 90% Muslim population, should been part of Pakistan, even though its ruler was a Hindu. But Nehru, who came from a family of Kashmiri Brahmins, would never had given it up, and the story of how India annexed it need not detain us here.

The tourist trade was at a standstill, and Aluddin and Shaila and I, for they were kind enough to allow me to join up with them, shared a fantastic houseboat. It was an enormous affair, with a huge lounge, dining room, and three large en suite bathrooms that would have graced a five star hotel. It had another attraction, having been occupied by the first President Bush when he visited India as a guest of the Indian Government a year or two previously.

With my father and mother, c.1927, prior to departure to India.

My mother in her late teens.

My father, probably at Capetown, South Africa.

With my in-laws. I am 2nd from the right in the front row, flanked by my cousins, and acutely embarrassed by my silk suit.

On the ship en route for India. Mother centre front row; Father back left.

A happy day in India.

At the wheel of my first car.

Chewing sugar-cane.

Important day; my first topi (hat).

With my father in the gardens at Palermo, Sicily, c.1934.

My father in his house at Rangoon, where he was Deputy Collector.

Father in the garden at Brighton, wearing the plus-fours so useful for smuggling cigars from France.

A party on board ship en route for India; middle row on the left.

My father's house in Rangoon.

Scandal Point, Simla. Father's postcard.

Panorama of Dal Lake, Kashmir – 'Paradise on Earth'.

Dal Lake, Srinigar, Kashmir.

Mohan Chabba (on right) outside the house he was building at Lonavala in the Western Ghats.

Construction in progress.

Mohan Chabba (on right) supervising the foundations of his house at Lonavala.

With Indian friends, Lonavala, 1994.

The Palace of Baroda.

The Portuguese Fort at Daman, Gujarat, India. What people they were!

Marseille. My father's postcard.

Port Said. Steamer in the harbour. My father's postcard.

Inn at Chamonix, Switzerland. My father's postcard.

Aden. My father's postcard.

Promenade, Luzern. My father's postcard.

Paris. My father's postcard.

Fishing canoe, Colombo. My father's postcard.

Constantinople (as my father always called it, and so it is to me). My father's postcard.

Lake Leman. My father's postcard.

River view, Calcutta. My father's postcard.

Genova. My father's postcard.

Gordon Gardens, Colombo. My father's postcard.

It was a time-capsule of the thirties, being curiously like a miniature English country house grafted on to a floating Kashmiri hull, covered with the intricate carving for which Kashmir is famous. There was a visitor's book, from which we realised that only a few years previously one would have had to book months or years ahead.

The nights were filled with the sounds of gunfire in Srinigar, which was crawling with Indian troops and army vehicles parading around the streets with machine guns at the ready, and road blocks everywhere. Thanks to our Pathan taxi driver, we did manage to see Srinigar in the daytime, and the Shalimar gardens built by Jehangir for his wife Nur Jahan, 'Light of the world'. And we did get to Gulmarg and see the view my mother took with her Box Brownie. I am sad when I think of Kashmir today, and the human folly that has brought misery, poverty and death to the poor of that beautiful vale, once the playground of British India.

Before I leave the sub-continent, let me hover briefly over Colombo in 1944, and in particular, descend to the 'Club', that stronghold of sahibs and mem-sahibs, whisky and sodas, bars labelled 'Gentlemen Only', and obsequious bearers.

It is Saturday evening, and the Colombo Amateur Dramatic Society, that strangely British manifestation of empire-builders at play, are about to stage *Dangerous . . . Corner* by J. B. Priestley. At the front of the audience are six rows of empire builders and their wives, all in evening dress. Behind them, separated by a *cordon sanitaire* of several rows of empty chairs, are three rows of merchant seamen, of whom I am one. Our presence has been arranged by the Missions to Seamen padre, who organised a boat to go around the anchorage to pick us up, including a party from my ship, the *Samdel.*

The plot involves the usual tangle of infidelity and murder, and the drama chiefly centres around a lonely cottage amid the woods, where most of the illicit coupling takes place. At one point the leading man dramatically exclaims, 'Where is she, where is she?' The Merchant Navy officers present exchange apprehensive glances, and their fears are only too fully realised.

'In the f.....g cottage!' roars a chorus of Liverpool-Irish firemen and deck-hands.

But it only gets worse. 'What shall I do, what shall do!' he moans, and his distress is obviously not just acting. Back comes the inevitable advice, shouted from the back through cupped hands 'F... her while she's still warm, mate.'

It was very good of them to ask us but the snobbery was inexcusable. I still resent those empty rows, designed to separate merchant seamen from a row of expatriate tradesmen comfortably sitting out the war in Colombo, well out of the range of German and Japanese torpedoes.

Chapter 5

MAMMY-WAGONS, SNAKES, AND THE DARK CONTINENT

West Africa in 1957

IN 1955, AFTER COMPLETING my three years in Pakistan, I returned to the UK for three weeks leave. That, plus the three weeks local leave I had taken abroad, was all that was due to me. One of those three weeks had been swallowed up by a flying visit to the UK which I kept secret from the company. I feared that if they knew I could find the money to fly home they would conclude they were paying me more than they needed to in Pakistan, which would not have helped with my future plans to ask for a cost of living abroad raise.

I booked a flight on a BOAC 'Argonaut' which had started off in Australia and hopped its way via Darwin, Singapore, Calcutta and Delhi to Karachi. As soon as we took off the engine just outside my window began to cough, and at Bahrein we were delayed for six hours while they tinkered with it. At Damascus the same thing occurred, but this time we were put in a hotel overnight. After breakfast the next morning I was staring gloomily down from an upper window at the square below through a steady drizzle, and recollecting that somewhere I had read that Mohammed had turned away from a view of Damascus from the hill of Salawyeh, lest he think no more of paradise. I reflected that Mohammed must have been luckier than I, but then he had not travelled there by BOAC!

Just under the window was a solitary human presence in the square in the form of a food vendor whose premises consisted of a wooden contraption with glass sides skilfully fitted with two bicycle wheels and handles to push it along. On top, and exposed to the elements, was a coke-heated samovar, presumably containing coffee or soup.

He was taking advantage of the rain to wipe down the sides of his cart with a dirty cloth, and after a quick look around to see that nobody was noticing, he would wring the cloth out into the samovar, presumably to compensate for the ullage created by the last customer.

The next stop was at Beirut, where we were delayed for a mere six hours before taking off for Nicosia in Cyprus. By this time the passengers were in a state of mutiny, but little did they know that worse was still to come. We took off from Nicosia with a full load of fuel for the longest hop of the flight, which was to Naples, and no sooner than we were in the air the port engine burst into flames. The passenger next to me, a Swiss commercial traveller in watches, starting shouting, while the air-hostess, courageous girl that she was, did her best to calm everybody.

The second pilot appeared, white-faced, but well in control of himself, and attempted to reassure us. 'Look,' he said, pointing out of the window, 'the flames are going out – we have switched on the fire-extinguishers. Can you see those clouds of vapour trailing behind us? We have to ditch the fuel before we can land.'

We spent the next twenty-four hours in Cyprus while they flew the plane back to Beirut on three engines to have a replacement fitted. At least there was a plus, for we were put up at the Dome Hotel in Kyrennia in the north of the island – the island had not then been divided up between Turkey and Greece. Kyrennia is an historic port overlooked by a fantastic Crusader castle, and I got a taxi to take me up to see it. The Turkish driver was a quaintly original ideologist, who spent most of the time explaining that private cars should be banned from the island, because they were wreaking havoc with the taxi business.

Mechanically, the rest of the flight was without incident, but still the jinx persisted, for at Frankfurt we were held up by severe snow storms and had to spend the night in a hotel. I remember that it was the first time I had encountered a duvet and spending a long time unbuttoning the cover under the impression it was a German variation on a sheet, and trying to crawl inside it. Eventually, I gave up, and accidentally used it the way it was intended.

Just before we landed in London the air-hostess, charming and efficient girl that she was, with a wry smile, handed all the passengers the standard BOAC form: 'Have you any suggestions that might improve the service?'

It might, in the year 2002, be remarked that three weeks leave after three years service abroad is the reverse of generous. To that my answer is 'Give me yesterday!'

I was young, glad of the opportunity to show what I could do given a chance, and in those three years in Pakistan I was able to save £1,800, which was enough to buy a four bedroomed detached house with a garage and a nice garden in a pleasant residential part of Wallasey, in the Wirral. It seems hard to realise now that there once was a time when if young people rolled up their sleeves and went to work, they could achieve things. Now they have to purvey nightmare music, play football, or operate in the tormented business world of E-mail, 'downsizing', and fat cat bosses.

At the end of my leave, instead of being sent back to India, where I had secret hopes of eventually being appointed manager of either the Bombay or Calcutta office, I was dispatched to West Africa, there to set up the Marconi Marine organisation. I was just thirty-one years old.

Typically, the company had no fixed idea of where to start – Lagos in Nigeria seemed the obvious choice to begin with, so I was told to go up to Liverpool, where all the main UK ship-owners who ran down to the West were situated, and find out what they thought. The consensus was that I should go out and see what the local opinion was, so I duly sailed on the Elder Dempster cargo-passenger liner *Sherbro*, with a case of instruments and a Marconi cheque-book.

It did not take me long to find an office, acquire a car, a

receptionist, and one general factotum, and from the beginning I was inundated with work – hands-on repairs on ships as well as sales and generally showing the company's flag. To begin with I had a flat out at Ikeja, near the airport, a place I generally saw for eight hours a day while I was sleeping. On Sundays I had longer, but that was if I was lucky. Ikeja was a twenty minute drive, even through Lagos traffic, and I gather it now takes three times as long, and is extremely dangerous; you are lucky to get from one end to the other without being car-jacked and robbed, and after dark, attacked into the bargain.

How different were things then! It is a refrain I keep coming back to throughout this book, and I apologise to the reader, for it serves no purpose. Lagos, in those pre-independence days, was a garden city, with wide clean roads, its racecourse, and comfortable residential areas. Above all, it was safe. Nigeria at that time was held up as the colonial country most likely to succeed; oil had not been discovered, and its rural economy amply kept the country ticking over. Cocoa and coffee beans were its backbone, and if the mammy-wagons and produce-laden river rafts were anything to go by, a substantial part of the population were happy and enjoyed the benefit of reasonable law and order. In fact it was not so different to the '*Sanders of the River*', where the British administration contained to a large extent the endemic religious and tribal tensions which have and are continuing to wreak such damage to Nigeria today.

During the whole of my eighteen months in West Africa, I worked an average of twelve hours a day, often more, and slept the rest. Lagos even then was a busy port, and my job was to repair anything electronic – communication, navigational, radar, or control equipment, of any manufacture, on ships of any nationality. And when I had dealt with all the ships in Lagos, there would be another batch in Takoradi, in neighbouring Ghana. It was my practice to be driven overnight across country to Accra, book in at the hotel there, and clear up whatever ships needed work done.

The port of Tema was then only in the process of being built, which meant going out by launch to ships lying at anchor. At that time ships were loaded and unloaded by surf-boats – wooden lighters paddled with incredible skill through the constant heavy surf by boatmen who over decades had developed it into an art form. Sometimes, I would return to Lagos on a ship bound there from Ghana and repair whatever needed it on the way around. And then the whole process began again. Between all this, I squeezed in sales and office work. The most recreation I allowed myself was to get mildly stewed on a Saturday night if there were no urgent jobs on hand, and sleep it off on Sunday. Yet, I look back to those eighteen months as one of the happiest periods of my life. What a thing it is was to be young, enthusiastic, and have something worthwhile to get one's teeth into!

In due course, the Marconi Marine depots at Accra and Freetown followed, and I like to think that I played some useful part in those countries' road to independence. I have no accurate knowledge of what their situation is now, but I cannot resist mentioning that an educated Sierra Leone friend who visited me five years ago remarked very seriously that nothing would please the average citizen of Freetown more than to again be under British colonial rule.

The main disadvantage to life in West Africa for me were the poisonous snakes, which abounded everywhere, and the horrible combination of baking heat and torrential rain. Nature seems to run wild; one's possessions rot easily; if you drop a pineapple core on the ground a few days later a new tree is springing into life.

One drawback was having to fly by West African Airways, and here I hasten to add that I am talking of forty-five years ago, when occasionally wings would fall off, or an engine become detached from the fuselage. Once, when passing through the lounge in Accra, there was a group of mechanics repairing an aeroplane engine, conveniently (for the mechanics) near to the restaurant and bar. But I am sure things are different now. At least I hope so.

In Karachi I knew several pilots who had found it necessary to leave BOAC rather suddenly, and who were extremely good company in the club. But it was with mixed feelings that I met one of these cheery soldiers of fortune in the bar at Accra airport before a flight back to Lagos. He was an old acquaintance of mine and sat chatting to a pretty girl perched on a bar stool displaying the most delectable knees. We had a chat about happy times in the bar at Karachi airport, with bacon and egg suppers to follow. Then I glanced at my watch and remarked that it was nearly time for my plane to take off. My friend glanced at his, and drained his glass. 'Yes,' he remarked, 'it's time we set off,' and marched across the tarmac to the waiting Dove aircraft, accompanied by the pretty girl, who turned out to be the only other member of the crew.

It was ten years before I visited West Africa again, and that was in order to find a character called Kelly, who was at the time the manager of the Marconi Marine depot in Freetown. It was standard practice for all the company's overseas depots to submit a monthly report to Head Office, and the first sign of anything wrong would of course show up in these reports, and if one failed to materialise warning bells began to ring all over Chelmsford. When two months had gone by without a report from Freetown, it was decided I should fly out to West Africa to investigate things on the spot, and call at Nigeria and Ghana while I was on the coast.

In the event, it took me two days to locate Kelly, even in a little place like Freetown, because he had, as they say out there, 'gone bush'. It was the classic recipe for disaster; overwork, and seeking refuge in a bottle. When I finally tracked him down he was in the early stages of D.T.s and sharing a room with huge green snakes and pink elephants.

The shipping agents, who were our main customers in Freetown, had begun to notice the deterioration in service, but had delayed complaining hoping that Kelly, whom they liked, would get himself back on the rails. Most of them were ex-seafarers, and sympathetic, but the situation couldn't have gone on much longer, or their own necks would have been on the line.

I managed to dry Kelly out sufficiently to get him on a plane to the UK. It was a depressing experience; he was about the same age as myself, and I liked him, and I was glad to get away from Freetown as soon as his relief arrived a few days later. I remark elsewhere in this book that Africa for me, below the Sahara, is always 'The Dark Continent', as it was for Joseph Conrad: 'Mr Kurtz, him dead!'

Chapter 6

ARABS, KASBAHS, AND *VIN ORDINAIRE*

North Africa, as seen from the sea

NORTH AFRICA FOR ME is a long straggling coastline of sun-baked ports with white houses set upon hills overlooking the Mediterranean, which appear idyllic from the sea.

Ashore, they are filled with dust, flies, goats and chickens whose diet seems to consist of old cigarette packets and fag-ends which had not been salvaged for re-fashioning into anonymous cigarettes which are sold loose, along with Spanish Fly, dirty postcards and leather goods manufactured from camel-hide. But also there is the delicious all-pervading fragrance of oranges, lemons, dates, cloyingly sweet liquers, and *vin ordinaire*. I had a sense of romance in the air, as if at any moment Beau Geste might come marching past, on his way to Fort Zinderneuf and Hollywood immortality among the sand-dunes and oases of the Sahara Desert.

But of course such recollections are of experiences when the tide of life was running like a torrent and adventure was in the air. In trying to recapture them on paper more than half a century later it is like the difference between seeing a dragon-fly hovering in the attic air, and the same thing pinned to a dusty card in a museum showcase.

North Africa began for me in 1942 when I joined my first ship, the *Ocean Viscount* in of all places, Swansea, where I now live. I presented myself at the office of the Marconi International Marine Company in Walter Road, which I now pass nearly every day. Although over the last twenty-five years it has been occupied by various businesses, the front door is still painted in the company's distinctive dark blue. Exactly twenty years later when I became – by the mysterious operation of inscrutable fortune – Personnel and Operations Manager of the entire company, and responsible for a sea staff of over 3,000 Radio Officers, the entire world-wide shore organisation, Operations, Traffic, and Training, I visited it again, under somewhat different circumstances.

The *Ocean Viscount* was a standard wartime ship, of the many built in North America to replace the catastrophic U-boat sinkings which decimated allied shipping during the first years of World War II, and incidentally claimed the lives of 980 Marconi Marine Radio Officers alone.

The 'Ocean' ships, so called because they were prefixed thus, were built at the Kaiser shipyards in Richmond, California, and were rapidly constructed on what until then had been a deserted mud flat. To Henry Kaiser must be due a substantial part of the credit for defeating Hitler, and in particular, Admiral Doenitz and his submarines. He also built the 'Liberty' ships, all with typical American flair and named after distinguished Americans, while those which sailed under the Red Ensign were prefixed 'Sam', and I served on two them, the *Samakron* and *Samdel*.

It gave me some amusement during a visit to San Francisco in March 1999 to research my book, *The Swansea Copper Barques & Cape Horners*. The maritime museum there has a tourist attraction in the form of the *Jeremiah O'Brian*, said to be the only working Liberty ship left afloat, and I went around it with a friend who came up from Los Angeles to meet me. The not-so-old-salt on the gangway had many blood-curdling tales to tell of U-boat sinkings, to which I listened with a suitably awed expression, while my friend did her best not to giggle. One of the amusements of being illusory, quite apart from all the other spin-offs, is listening politely to stories you know from your own experience to be untrue, but not revealing it.

Sir Richard Burton, the Victorian explorer, linguist, translator, poet, swordsman and writer, was scarcely an illusion, but incorporated so many persons in one individual he might be considered a variation on the theme, used to tell people that nothing afforded him greater amusement than to be disbelieved when he was telling the truth. There is a complicated train of thought here, and perhaps I am in danger of getting lost, but I know what he meant, and I think there is a moral here somewhere.

To return to Henry Kaiser. With typical transatlantic dynamism he broke through traditional shipbuilding methods by substituting welding for rivetting, and prefabricating whole sections of ships, so that they could be built anywhere, even in places remote from the sea. I remember the wise ones shaking their heads and prophesying that these ships would fall to pieces within five years. Twenty-five years later they were still ploughing the seas under all kinds of flags, though admittedly most had been strengthened by longitudinal rivetting.

I remember that before sailing I went with some others from the ship to the 'Bush', an old established public house in High Street, Swansea, which had not then been transmogrified into its later status as a chain steak-house. Then it had atmosphere, still with a lingering flavour of the old sailing ship days of the Swansea copper barques.

I never pass it now without thinking of how it was in 1942, filled with sea-farers, dockers, cigarette smoke, talk, and laughter. And like other old Swansea pubs, what tales could those old polished mahogany bars have told if they could speak. And how many during World War II sailed from Swansea and never returned.

Two days afterwards I was standing on the wing of the bridge feeling seasick and peering over the side when I saw a round dark metal object with protruding horns bobbing about in the oily grey swell of the Bristol Channel. The second Mate, Lloyd Imber, whose name has remained in my memory for fifty-eight years, looked at me and grinned wryly. 'It's a mine,' he said.

We arrived, loaded with tanks and ammunition for the Eighth Army at my first foreign port at sea, Algiers, and it seems only yesterday that I had my first sight of a jostling North African quayside, crowded with Arab dock-workers and British soldiers and sailors. In the town there were mountains of oranges and lemons for sale and every other business seemed to be a bar selling vino and liquers. German bombers were active, and every so often there would be an air-raid warning, and the sound of anti-aircraft guns blazing away from the merchant and naval ships in the harbour, mostly firing holes in each other's funnels! But the noise they made comforted us; we felt we were doing something.

My memories of those North African ports – Saffi, Oran, Algiers, Bizerta, Tunis, Sfax, and Alexandria – all share a common denominator. Viewed from the sea, dazzling white buildings set off against patches of green vegetation, and bathed in sunshine. Ashore, smells, dirt, emaciated horses dragging broken-down gharries, goats, dung everywhere, and Arabs either asleep on the ground oblivious of flies crawling all over them, or endeavouring to sell souvenirs and pick your pockets at the same time.

They used to say that the pick-pockets in the Khan Kalali, the main bazaar in Cairo, were so skilful that before the war they could remove the trousers of an American tourist and hang lead weights on his braces, so that he did not realise they were gone. Of course, this is a wicked exaggeration, but still not a million miles from the truth. Not that Cairo has a monopoly in this respect. I read that there was a time when a well-dressed man could not walk the length of the Portobello Road and emerge intact at the other end. In later years, when I was sent on business to the Middle East, a wise General Manager advised me to always make sure that I had two eyes left in my head after closing a deal – in case one had been removed without my noticing it!

Here I must declare myself an Arabist and do justice to my friends, especially if they are of the genuine desert variety. They are invariably polite and charming, and the best of company, and when it comes to hospitality they have no equal. The fact is that all over the Levantine and Middle East, and for that matter India, business and politics are universally conducted on the basis of bribery, and what appears to us to be corruption. But it is merely a different way of doing things. Our trouble is that in the West we try to impose our own mores on others, and then cry to heaven when we find that we have been taken to the cleaners.

I hope to deserve the gratitude of readers by not even briefly hovering over such worn themes as the war in the Mediterranean, visits to the Pyramids and Cairo Museum. Instead, I shall move on to 1968, when business took me once again to the Middle East as part of a tour that included Aden, Pakistan, India and East Africa.

It began in Cairo at the Nile Hilton Hotel, where I had a meeting with the owner of a well-known north-east coast shipping firm which had been appointed as technical advisers to a newly formed tanker company in Kuwait.

As a happy consequence of having to wait three days for a plane to Aden, my next stop, I spent three days in a cabana by the pool of the Hilton, which did me absolutely no harm at all. Also at the meeting was the manager of the Kuwaiti company, whom I shall refer to as Mr Ali K, to whom I had been introduced in London in order to learn the script of what was going to be required of me when I got to the Middle East.

I travelled out as far as Alexandria as a guest of Shell Tankers on the *Drupa*, which was at the time their commodore ship. Theoretically, I was to observe on the spot the practical operation of a new category of Radio Officer, which I had been personally responsible for introducing, called an Electronics Officer. This was a superior version of the standard Radio Officer, capable of maintaining all the electronic equipment on board.

In the event I enjoyed a pleasant break, where I was accommodated in the owner's room and spent most of my time gossiping with the Captain and officers in the ship's bar. He was a keen member of his local gun-club and liked to practice his marksmanship by massacring seagulls from the wing of the bridge.

The Master of a merchant ship is entitled to carry a revolver, and has exceptional powers conferred on him by law to use it in an emergency – a relic of the days when mutiny was a very real danger.

Essentially, the plot was that my company was keen to oblige the north-east shipping company owner, whom I shall call Mr C, in the hope of getting orders for our equipment. Mr C's company wanted to oblige Mr Ali K, who in turn had axes of his own to grind not entirely remote from his connection with the Ruler of Kuwait. My contribution, though not put into so many words, was to inspect my company's agencies in the Persian Gulf, and in the case of Kuwait, report unfavourably so that it could be transferred to a relative of Mr Ali K. I still wriggle with embarrassment when I remember with what courtesy the owner of our agency, a most charming and cultivated Arab gentleman, smilingly indicated that he was well aware of the purpose of my visit, and did his best to help me through our interview. It was an object lesson to me on how business is conducted in the Middle East, and I salute his memory and his contribution to the unravelling of my business immaturity.

It was the same with bribery, when my illusions in that respect were dispelled in the course of managing the Marconi Marine office in Karachi. I went to Pakistan with the idea that if anyone tried to bribe me I would throw the money in their face. I soon discovered that things are not always quite like that. For instance, I received a visit at Christmas time from the Parsee owner of a fleet of Pakistan registered ships who called in to thank me for my efforts. After he left, I found an envelope containing the equivalent of several hundred pounds in rupees on my desk. I had done nothing but provide the service he had paid for; it was simply a generous expression of appreciation of good work. Should I have gone to his office and returned it with indignation? Of course, I did nothing of the kind.

At a lower level, I had occasion to order new furniture for the office. In the Karachi of those days there were no furniture stores; everything was made specifically to one's order. The proprietor of the business, an old gentleman whose red beard proclaimed that he had gone on the Haj to Mecca, offered me some fringe benefits outside the transaction. I did not accept, but I have never forgotten his soporific explanation: 'But I am your friend, you are my friend, surely one friend can give another friend a present?'

I had a curious experience at the Nile Hilton, which I have never forgotten. I was dining with Mr Ali K and Mr C in a restaurant on the top floor, which had been done up to look like a sort of desert sheikh's tent, complete with a three man orchestra – a one-stringed fiddle, noisy cymbals, and a drum. A belly-dancer dressed in a filmy gauze (it was at that time under Nasser, when if you wanted a glass of whisky it was brought to you in a teapot with a cup and saucer) gyrated about on a small stage.

At the coffee and liqueur stage the house fortune-teller appeared at our table and offered to read our palms. She was strikingly beautiful, and could have been any age between twenty-five and fifty, with that flawless ivory complexion you find in Cairo women of mixed Arab and French descent. She had straight raven black hair and wore a very low cut black evening gown set off by a heavy gold necklace and matching ear-rings.

I wasn't very enthusiastic, but Mr Ali K pressed me to go ahead and not wishing to offend him I agreed, with the stipulation that she must first be told what she could of what had gone before in my life. I thought it would soon expose her to me, though I would leave it at that.

What happened next has remained with me ever since. I can see her now, a ravishing scented mixture of sexual attraction, the East, and the occult. She gave a little smile and grabbing both my hands turned them face upwards. Studying their shape and the mounts she gave an enigmatic smile which seemed to penetrate the depths of my being. Then she took my right hand, and peering at it closely without turning her head rattled off a bird's-eye summary of the main events of my previous life which was correct in every detail. She (this was in 1968) said that I would pass through times when all I would have left was courage, but emerge from them successful in the eyes of the world. And finally that I was destined to die in a far-off land, but surrounded by friends.

Of course, such predictions always contribute to their own fulfilment if one believes in such things. But so far it seems to be holding up. Whether the 'foreign land' refers to the UK in the sense that it is far off from Egypt I cannot say; only time will tell. All I can say is that from that day onwards I have never been uneasy in an aircraft or on a ship, though there have been several occasions when I was probably alone in that belief. The other consequence has been my study of cheiromancy, which I should explain concerns the whole hand, rather than its market-place cousin, palmistry, that dubious playground of charlatans and contributors to the popular press. This is not to say that the main lines of the hand do not have deep significance; they do, but here is not the place to go into more detail. I claim, however, that if I can look at an individual's hand closely it tells me most of what I need to know about him or her. I avoid telling people about their hands, because it is too important a topic for casual chatter. On the rare occasions when I am persuaded by my friends to talk about the subject, I find that they usually end up by sitting on their hands or putting them out of sight in their pockets.

At least I have the cheerful thought that if some disaster reduced me to indigence I need never starve. Some beads and a shawl would be the only capital required.

Mr Ali K was kind enough to invite me to what he called his 'beach house', which turned out to be a sumptuous establishment furnished on a lavish scale with every conceivable modern amenity, bordering the sea and situated amid gardens artificially sustained by incessant watering.

On arrival in Kuwait I had been met by a European employee of Mr Ali K's tanker company, who whisked me up to a hotel room where he produced a soft drink bottle filled with illegal whisky. He poured out two measures in tooth-glasses and all his troubles at the same time, and my sense of unease shot up the stratosphere when he confided that to be caught with alcohol in one's possession in Kuwait could lead to a period of breaking up stones in the local jail. This was interesting, because Mr Ali K, one of the most charming and hospitable men it has been my good fortune to meet, took me to his private bar, reminiscent of the long bar in Raffles Hotel in Singapore, complete with a barman and his assistant, and every alcoholic drink one could think of.

In the Arab world, society is driven by the concepts of honour and shame, and honour comes with lineage, age, and above all the possession of wealth. As the Moroccan historian, Al-Hajj Mohammed, exquisitely put it: 'If a rich man farts it is as though a canary had sung; if a poor man farts he is taken to the market place and beaten.'

Chapter 7

CONVOYS, U-BOATS, AND LEARNING TO PLAY STUD POKER

THE OTHER DAY, while researching for another book, I received a photograph from the Hull College of Technology which showed the equipment used to teach students on the marine radio course in 1931. I looked, and then looked again; and suddenly fifty-eight years dropped away. There, screwed on a bench, was all the equipment one could expect to see on a vessel of that period. On the left was a 1½ Kilowatt Valve Transmitter; then came a Direction-Finder, Two Valve Receiver, Auto-Alarm, and a ¼ Kilowatt Quench Gap Spark Transmitter. Under the bench and fixed to walls was a supporting assembly of motor-alternators, charging boards, and accumulators. Fascinated, I realised that I was looking, with the exception of the valve transmitter, at all the equipment fitted on the steam tramp *Lorca* which I joined early in 1943 in Middlesborough. As I write this it seems as yesterday, so clearly do I remember signing articles on a damp, freezing, foggy morning – the sort of weather with which the north-east coast regularly fortifies her children.

In those days ship's crews were signed on the Articles by the Master, under the supervisory eye of the Shipping Master. Like most shipping offices in the big ports the counter had a heavy brass grill screwed on its top; this was because the shipping clerks tended to be so superior and offensive to crews that it was necessary for their protection.

I signed as Chief Radio Officer, even though I was still only eighteen years old – so many Radio Officers had been lost since the war started that the authorities were scraping the bottom of the barrel. In wartime one grows up quickly, a blessing I have been thankful for all my life. Next morning we were steaming up the North Sea, bound for North Shields and Smith's Dry Dock, no junior Radio Officers being deemed necessary for the short trip.

The *Lorca* was what was termed a 'three-island ship' with a raised forecastle, well-deck hatches, midships accommodation for the officers and stewards, more well-deck hatches, and a raised after section. Owned by Cory Brothers, the north-east coast Coal and Bunkering Agents, she had like the rest of the Merchant Service been taken over by the Ministry of War Transport.

How fortunate I was to have experienced the *Lorca*! She was a mint specimen of her period, and the carpenter who sailed on her had worked on the ship when she was built, and been on her ever since. He had all sorts of anecdotes about the ship; one that I particularly remember was the electric bulb on the top of the foremast that had never needed changing since the ship was built.

The woodwork and brasswork in the accommodation was a sight to behold, heavy mahogany and polished brass everywhere. The Saloon, where the officers had their meals, and which also served as a social centre, was a mass of cut glass and gleaming mahogany.

Overhead hung two ornate brass lamps suspended in gimbals. All the cabins had brass lamps – 'Paraffin Dynamos', as we used to call them. The ship had electric light of course, but before the war this was generally shut down in port by the owner's orders, in order to save the coal which would be used by the donkey-engine generator.

The Saloon and Radio Room were heated by coal stoves called 'bogies'; the one in the Radio Room being much in demand for all the officers to hang their clothes around to dry after washing them in a bucket in the usual way.

The crew all lived in the forecastle which was divided in two; sailors on one side, and firemen on the other, and each had their own toilet facing aft. They tended to leave the doors open unless the weather was very bad because there was no electric light. My own cabin was a delight to me. It was situated on the port side with a big coaming over which one stepped straight out on to the deck. Right through the centre went a brass casing around the chimney from the saloon fire. I was always snug but got burned when heavy weather threw me against it.

I cannot remember what cargo we loaded after leaving North Shields; probably we went out light ship, for the purpose of the ship was to load manganese ore at Pepel, which lay up the river above Freetown.

From the Tyne we sailed north about to the convoy gathering point, which in that case was Loch Ewe. There I went ashore with the Master, he to the Master's conference, I to the Radio Officers. There, along with the others I was briefed on what codes and special signals would be employed by the convoy Commodore in the event of U-boat attacks, and it was explained that the convoy would take a wide sweep out into the south Atlantic before heading in for the convoy gathering point at Freetown.

There were either 10 knot or 7½ knot convoys, and ours was a slow one. The big passenger liners, then serving as troop-ships, could travel at their own speed, which protected them from submarine attack anyway. I shall never forget glimpsing a group of them, dimly outlined against a misty dawn horizon, steaming at full speed, escorted by destroyers. At the convoy conference the Briefing Officer had stressed the importance of a vigilant wireless watch for signals from the Commodore, informing us that ships loaded with ore – as the *Lorca* would be – would, if torpedoed in the Number 1 or 2 hatches, be likely to just carry on steaming straight down under the surface. Only those on the bridge or on deck would have any chance at all in waters that were infested with sharks which followed ships in order to feed on the galley refuse thrown overboard.

The manganese wharf at Pepel was a day's steaming up the Sierra Leone River, around twisting bends along a swirling, muddy waterway, lined with dense tropical forest which wound its way into the heart of the Dark Continent. What you get in that part of the world is a combination of insufferable heat, drenching rain, the ship becomes a sort of furnace, and the perspiration which pours off you seems to cling to the skin and smell. There is something about Africa which I have never liked, which I cannot define rationally. I think it springs from my youthful recollection of that river. I have a sense of innate corruptibility and hostility to fair society which sadly seems to neutralise the efforts of that minority of European-educated idealists vainly trying to bring order and an end to the endemic corruption that afflicts black Africa.

I still have vivid memories of the old *Lorca*. It was on her in my late teens that I learned to play pontoon, solo-whist and stud poker, sitting at the long green-baize covered saloon table. The Chief Engineer was a great one for cards. He had a huge belly that he could scarcely wedge in front of the table, which he used to pat, and shout: 'Forty years of wasted life!' But his life wasn't wasted; those old time Chief Engineers knew everything about their job, from turning up something on the lathe to weighing sacks of coal.

Across the years I salute my old friends, and gratefully acknowledge how much I owe to them. I see them now across a distance of more than fifty years, very clearly, but as if they are a long way off, like looking through the wrong end of a telescope. And what I remember is not the U-boats and the sinkings, but crowding around in each other's cabins with a case of twenty-four cans of Barclays beer on the floor, the air thick with cigarette smoke and telling the hoary old jokes that everybody knew by heart but never tired of telling, and above all, the laughter.

Chapter 8

THE BRIEF-CASE YEARS

THINKING ABOUT THIS chapter set me on a fruitless search for a risqué postcard I once acquired in Brussels during a business trip in the 1960s. It depicted a skinny, worried-looking business man in a pin-striped suit sitting on a toilet with his trousers around his ankles, and balancing a brief-case and a bowler hat on his bony knees. The caption underneath read: 'The only man in Head Office who knows what he is doing'.

It is a mental picture that invariably comes to my mind whenever that hilarious yet pathetic business growth, the Senior Executive, enters my field of vision. I do not of course refer to the Fat Cats, those modern-day robber barons, who live in bogus Elizabethan mansions in Sunningdale, far from their industrialised peasantry toiling in factories or pushing paper about in offices. For ten years I was an executive, but I was never quite in thrall like the other occupants of a row of offices at the top of the Head Office building, which housed the Managing Director and his court of Divisional Managers. It was a thickly carpeted area, where ordinary folk spoke in hushed tones, and wondered what it was like beyond the sacred entrance to the Imperial Toilets, which appropriately was raised on a sort of dais approached by a series of wide steps. But I think I was protected by a constant sense of participating in a sort of charade in which I did not find it difficult to perform my part.

It was my good fortune to be injected into this charmed circle at an early age from the rough and tumble of a life at sea, followed by fourteen years of hands-on challenges against various backgrounds in different parts of the world. 'By indignities, men come to dignities,' so wrote Sir Francis Bacon with bitter truth.

Along that painful way I had learned the value of the ignominious practice of feeding back to people what I knew they wanted to hear. But above all I made myself useful to whoever was immediately above me, but without threatening that individual, and making sure that he got all the credit. It was a golden formula, which projected me upwards, just as I never asked for a rise for myself – only for whoever was below me on the ladder. These are not nice confessions and it was not until long after I shook the dust of being an executive from under my feet that I could work off the Karma of those years. It is much easier to be virtuous once one is out of the rat race. And I was only thirty-eight.

I have described the Marconi International Marine Communication Company at some length in my book, *The History of the Radio Officer in the British Merchant Navy and on Deep-Sea Trawlers* (alas, I could not get it any shorter!). Here I will sum it up as supplying wireless equipment and Radio Officers to ships and providing a radio-telegraph accounting service.

In the beginning these services were only offered by the company on a rental-maintenance basis, which included the hire of a Radio Officer, who was employed by the company.

This was possible because the Marconi Marine Company, founded in April 1900 by Guglielmo Marconi, was a monopoly and held all the patents. Marconi is commonly referred to as the inventor of wireless communication at sea, but in fact that is not true. His genius was to translate the discoveries of Maxwell, Hertz, Edouard Branly and Sir Oliver Lodge into a practical system of communication without wires – wireless telegraphy.

When I went to work at Head Office in Chelmsford fifty-eight years later the presence of Marconi still brooded over the factory and offices in New Street. The chandeliers which hung over the executive lunch table, to which I later graduated, had shone down upon the gastronomic activities of the Master himself. Transistors had not yet been invented and components were mounted on a metal chassis and everything held together by nuts and bolts.

On my return from West Africa, draped in youthful laurels, I was still hoping to be sent back to India as Manager of either the Bombay or Calcutta office. Instead, I was told that I was destined for greater things, and appointed Assistant Manager of the company's Operating and Traffic Division at Head Office in Chelmsford. This looked after about 2,500 Radio Officers employed in the Merchant Navy and another 400 on deep-sea trawlers, as well as all the company's radio traffic operation and accounting.

The manager, who had joined the company in 1908, operated largely in a time warp, and welcomed me with the comment that he would endeavour not to hold against me what he described, perhaps correctly, as my bubble reputation. I was irritated, more so because I knew that he had only actually been manager of the division for less than a year, having played second fiddle to his predecessor, who had been Assistant General Manager of the whole company, for more than forty years.

However, I hung on his words and listened respectfully to his interminable stories so successfully that I became bathed in the glow of his approbation. On his belated retirement (he clung like a barnacle onto the job for two years after normal retirement age), I thankfully mounted the dais, and once again became my own person.

It was then that I found out that the higher up one gets on the ladder, the easier life becomes. You can pick the wits of people below you and steal their ideas. So often they are brighter and more intelligent, but lack that mysterious quality for getting on, which can only be described as a gift from Heaven, though there may be more than a whiff of the Lord of the Underworld about it as well.

Above a certain level, you can achieve miracles with business jargon, an accomplishment at which our American cousins have achieved near perfection. In fact, they can conduct a conversation entirely in jargon, while another part of their mind is engaged on how they are going to make the next undeclared dollar, or seduce their best friend's wife. What I mean is perfectly demonstrated by the following formula for creating instant buzz-words, for which I am indebted to Molly Izzard, in her fascinating book, *The Gulf*:

THE BUZZ-PHRASE GENERATOR

0	Integrated	0	Management	0	Options
1	Overall	1	Organised	1	Flexibility
2	Systemised	2	Monitored	2	Capability
3	Parallel	3	Reciprocal	3	Mobility
4	Functional	4	Digital	4	Programming
5	Responsive	5	Logistical	5	Concept
6	Optimal	6	Transitional	6	Time-phase
7	Synchronised	7	Incremental	7	Projection
8	Compatible	8	Third-generation	8	Hardware
9	Balanced	9	Policy	9	Contingency

Proceed as follows: Think of a three-digit number at random and take the corresponding word from each column. Thus, 601 gives you 'Optional Management Flexibility'. This generator will confer on its users instant expertise, enabling them to invest anything they write, not with any particular meaning, but that desirable ring of decisive, progressive, knowledgeable authority.

(Acknowledgement: Mr John G. Pike of the Food & Agriculture Organisation of the United Nations).

I am typing these words on an all-singing all-dancing modern computer, which is connected to the internet should I desire to expose my life to the slavery of E-mail, which I don't. When puzzled friends ask why I am such a stick in the mud, I answer that I do not want to spend a large part of each day answering a multitude of E-mails. It is a mystery to me how it is possible for today's business executives to deal efficiently with dozens, if not hundreds, of E-mails each day. The answer must be that they cannot, which is why so many companies are in trouble, while their unfortunate executives grow ulcers on their ulcers as they become ever submerged in paper.

During the 1960s a pile of correspondence a foot high used to arrive for my division. It was sorted out by my secretarial people into the three sections into which the division was divided. Routine letters and memoranda were intercepted by my secretary and never reached my desk. What was left I would mark out for the section heads with what I wanted done, and the balance would appear on my desk, each with the relevant file of previous correspondence which I could glance at before dictating a reply.

Today, I would require a desk the size of a snooker table to deal with things in that way, yet how else can it be efficiently done? I suppose the answer is that I am an example of an extinct species. In the days of the old East India Company if you got a letter from Leadenhall Street, you could raise a query, secure in the knowledge that the answer would not reach you for another year. Wonderful! It is all relative, like the boy at Eton who said: 'My people are very, very poor. But our butler is even poorer.'

I still have in my possession a copy of the first 'General Orders' for Radio Officers, dated 1907. It is a vintage piece, which could almost have been written by Ebenezer Scrooge for the guidance of Bob Cratchett. For instance, take Rule 6 – Staff records:

> 'At the Head Office of the Company a staff record of every operator is kept, in which all particulars regarding the general conduct and manner in which telegraphic and clerical duties have been carried out, are recorded – special attention being given to the observance or non-observance of the Company's regulations. The remarks and entries made in each staff record are taken into full account when the annual increments are under consideration.'

And Rule 12:

> 'Telegraphists should remember that they are not in any way entitled to leave of absence as a right, but that it is a privilege to be earned by attention to duty and general good work. Generally, 14 days leave of absence, per annum, will be granted to each operator.'

The book also lays down the Radio Officer's responsibilities in the care of the equipment in his charge and watch-keeping duties. It then goes on to specify in excruciating detail everything to do with wireless traffic, down to last half-penny.

Rule 38. Watch-Keeping Duties:

> 'The instruments shall not be left unattended during working hours. At all stations provided with two or more operators a continuous watch is insisted upon. Any breach of this regulation will be regarded seriously'.

At least Rule 43 provides some light relief:

> 'Should it be brought to the Company's notice that any operator has been guilty of using profane or abusive language in connection with his duties, he will be INSTANTLY DISMISSED.'

In 1963, when I became responsible for the whole of the company's staff, including Radio Officers, one of my first and most agreeable tasks was to re-write the 'General Orders'.

I had wanted to do this when I first went to Chelmsford, but to my predecessor, the 'General Orders' had been brought down from the mountain. His favourite remark when making a judgement was: 'There is no point in having rules if they are not strictly enforced.' He was of the oak, rather than the willow!

For example, if a Radio Officer undercharged a radio-telegram by a half-penny he would receive a letter from Head Office pointing out this grave dereliction of duty and informing him that the amount would be deducted from his salary, and a 'note made in your staff record'. If, however, it was an over-charge, usually no action would follow unless the amount was so large as to expose the company to criticism if it came to light later.

As early as the 1920s competition came from other manufacturers of wireless equipment; rival radio companies developed, though not employing Radio Officers in the numbers of Marconi

Marine, and some shipowners began to realise that it was cheaper and more satisfactory to employ their Radio Officers directly. In the 1960s this trickle became a flood which turned into a torrent in the '70s. By then satellite communication was rendering the Radio Officer obsolete, and by the end of the '80s it was all over. The gravy train finally hit the bumpers.

But it was a wonderful racket while it lasted. The simple equipment of the 1920s, '30s, and '40s probably earned their capital cost in the first year's rental; the rest was sheer profit, though it steadily became less as the gear became more complicated. But the biggest income came from what Mr Arthur Daley would have described as a 'nice little earner'. Until the 1970s, Radio Officers were employed on a voyage basis, i.e. they were not paid until they signed off at the end of a voyage, which could be up to two years. During this period Radio Officers could leave an allotment to wives or dependants, but a certain amount of money always had to be left on the ship. Advances could be obtained from the company's various depots, but this was not encouraged, especially abroad. The consequence of this happy arrangement was that the company at any one time had a massive sum of interest-free money at its disposal, already earned by Radio Officers, and owing to them. It formed a major if concealed part of the company's profits and as the number of Radio Officers employed by the company declined, so did its viability, threatened as it was by severe technical competition.

By the early part of 1971 this depressing situation was becoming increasingly clear to me. The Marconi Marine Company was renowned for its meagre salaries and accounting procedures, which had evolved during its early monopolistic days, such as expecting all rental-maintenance payments to be paid three months in advance, while its bills were paid three months in arrears or less depending on who was owed the money. For years I had known that Radio Officers at sea could earn very much more than the shore staff, and this combined with the general situation and my own personal considerations prompted me to hand in my resignation, which was accepted with alacrity. Two years later I returned to sea for ten happy years, and right from the start my earnings at sea were almost double what I received as Personnel and Operating Manager of the Marconi Marine Company.

The years in management had been full of interest and travel. I had served on important committees, been a member of UK government delegations abroad, and for ten years a major voice in the field of marine radio and electronics. Yet through it all I had just been play-acting; performing to an audience. And it was a relief when the performance was over.

The social side of those years seems in retrospect to be equally unreal. For about five years during the mid '60s I was sucked into what I might describe as the outer fringes of the county set. It began when I moved from Chelmsford to Mistley, on the south bank of the Stour, roughly opposite to Flatford Mill and the Constable country. There I bought a house called Park Lodge which had previously been the family home of the owners of Edme Maltings, the brewers, who I believe later became Ind-Coope.

It was a large brick late Georgian house built in the shape of a crucifix, with extensive matured grounds, a small wood, a large paddock, and a range of those outbuildings and greenhouses without which a Victorian gentleman's house was incomplete. French windows looked out on to a quarter of an acre of lawn with a magnificent beech tree in the middle, and a thatched Edwardian child's playhouse. On one side was a row of ancient fruit trees covered with mistletoe, for that was how Mistley got its name – the Mistlewoods.

It was approached by a semi-circular drive ending on either side by white-painted double gates, fringed by rose gardens and huge eucalyptus trees. At any moment, so to speak, one might expect the author of *Alice Through the Looking Glass*, or Edward Fitzgerald to come sauntering in from the woods holding a book of poetry. There was even a lavish Victorian darkroom, complete with sinks and taps.

I had no time to attend to this demesne, which would have

become a wilderness had it not been for Sydney, a middle-aged man who had suffered a learning disability in his childhood, in the days when that was confused with semi-idiocy. He lived in a local home and was allowed out to do gardening, at which he excelled. Sydney was never happier than when he was weeding, sweeping up leaves, and above all, lighting bonfires. I soon discovered that he had a wonderful affinity with living things, plant and animal, and there was little wrong with his brain that might not have been much improved by education. Realising this I arranged a sort of literary menu, for he could read children's books, and eventually got him up to *Robinson Crusoe* and *Treasure Island*. One of the great achievements of my life was to arrange with the superintendent of the home to allow him to go to Ipswich on the bus to see a football match, and when I sold the Park Lodge it was on the understanding that he was kept on as a gardener.

I had not been in Mistley very long before my neighbour, a retired farmer, whose wife was a local JP, approached me to attend a meeting in the village hall intended to set up a local preservation society. I duly went along and found the place filled with characters straight out of St Mary Mead, including a respectful row of villagers at the rear, for a distinctly pre-war atmosphere still hung about Mistley and the contiguous village of Manningtree.

I was only dimly following the proceedings, for in those days I was always half asleep after getting home from the office. Suddenly, I realised to my horror that my neighbour, Sydney Webb, without having asked me first, was proposing me as the first Chair of the Manningtree and District Amenity Society. Frantically, I got up and began to mumble that I was a newcomer to the village, and had an occupation that took me all over world, never mind only being able to spend a small proportion of my waking hours in Mistley. It was to no avail, for my neighbour, who was sitting next to me, explained that was exactly why they wanted me – someone with a non-parochial outlook, and that there would only be one meeting a month. In any case, he added, all the real work would be done by the secretary, a lady who proved to be charming, accomplished, indefatigable, and able to move mountains.

And as I realised later, that is how these things are done. As if by magic a platoon of local gentry, some with handles to their names, appeared as Vice-Presidents, who prattled gaily about 'Dear Randolph', Winston Churchill's son, who lived on the other side of the Stour, and who was a local by-word for rudeness to everyone outside his charmed circle.

From there it was a short step to be invited to serve on the Manningtree and District Council. Again I protested, explaining that I had no time to attend meetings and certainly not to canvas votes. But canvassing, it was explained to me, would not be necessary, three seats were always reserved for appointment without popular franchise, and meetings were only once a month, and if I could not make it that would not be a problem. In a mad moment I agreed, and from then on things went from bad to worse. Village people came knocking on the door asking me to sign things or support their applications for charity, or lend my name to something or other.

There was a second-hand furniture dealer in the village who decided to set himself up as an estate agent, and approached me to sign his application for membership of some body which awarded professional qualifications in the house selling business without the formality of an examination. It had an impressive acronym, and I wished him well so I signed it. He was an excellent junk dealer; I had previously bought all sorts of useful items from him – Welsh-dressers and pianos at thirty shillings each, and so on, which today sell for thousands. And I am sure he made a first-class estate agent. But it was not long before I realised that I had not entered the charmed circle, and anyway the more I saw of it the less I wished to be enveloped in the magic dust. I was being picked up, and just as easily would be put down. I was an actor in a play whose theme I was not suited to. After three years I laid down my weary local burdens, sold Park Lodge, and went to live in a Tudor farmhouse called Poplar Farm a few miles north of Ipswich.

Joanna at the Gateway to India, Bombay, prior to the drive from Bombay to Amritsar in the Punjab.

A roadside accident in India; a common event.

The Golden Temple, Amristar, India.

Palace at Jaipur.

Dhows at Suez.

The Writer's Building from Dalhousie Square, Calcutta. My father's postcard.

Port Stanley, Falkland Islands 1982/3.

The four minarets of the Taj Mahal (1654) at Agra.

The cenotaphs in the Taj Mahal at Agra.

S.S. Lorca.

Convoy World War II.

An illicit photograph I took in 1943.

Caught alone in the South Atlantic.
(Photograph: H.M.S.O.).

A magazine illustration which shows the sort of equipment I first went to sea with.

The Baxtergate (pre-war photograph).

M.V. Nacella (in pre-war colours).

Joanna Greenlaw (fifth from the right from RSS de L'Ukraine) while serving as a member of the UK delegation to the International Telecommunication Union at Geneva, 1958.

TO LICENSED and OTHER PERSONS.

TAKE NOTICE

That under the 26th and 27th Clauses of the Licensing Ordinance, (Cap. 38.) I have this day made an Order in Court prohibiting any person, whether Licensed or otherwise, from giving or selling to, or purchasing or procuring for PAUL VIVIAN GREENLAW LINTZGY any intoxicating liquor whatsoever for the space of 18 MONTHS from this date, under pain of being dealt with as prescribed by the said Ordinance.

Given under my hand and Seal of the Court, at Stanley, this EIGHTH day of FEBRUARY 19 83

Senior Magistrate.

Souvenirs of my time as Chief Radio Officer of the troop-ship 'St Edmund', eight months (1982/3) in the south Atlantic and Flakland Islands.

The officers of the 'St Edmund', 1982. Joanna Greenlaw, in previous mode, middle back row behind Master.

The hulk of one of the few East Indiamen at Port Stanley, 1982.

The 'Ocean Viscount', taken just after the war.

The 'Samdel'. A Liberty ship, taken just after the war.

The 'Marilock' on which I spent eighteen happy months, including one round the world voyage.

The 'St Edmund'.

Joanna Greenlaw in reflective mood, while trekking in the lower Himalayas, 1995.

Poplar Farm had been built in 1490 and had (with all the buildings, including thatched barns, that went with a three hundred acre dairy herd) been run by its previous owner, a Miss Van Moppe, the daughter of a Hatton Graden diamond merchant. I only had the buildings and about twelve acres of paddocks, orchards and ponds – for there were ponds everywhere. The house, one room deep, with leaded Tudor windows, had been built, so to speak, on the spot, from local materials, and rose up on a base of elm logs, a structure of oak and plaster.

The clay had been dug up on the site, creating the ponds in the process, which formed a connected system linked to a sluggish stream that meandered across it. There was scarcely a level floor in the entire structure, and the chimney-breast in the centre of the house was the only place where bricks had been used. It rose up from the ground floor through three stories, to be surmounted by an Elizabethan chimney of intricately decorated brickwork. At the bottom it opened upwards from two huge open hearths, feeding the two main rooms of the house on either side of the chimney breast, which could accommodate a Yule log of Washington Irving proportions.

Miss Moppe had been a little eccentric, wrapped up in her herd of pedigree Jersey cows, and one of the main ground floor rooms, which had French windows which were left permanently open so that it could be freely used by chickens and the ornamental ducks which I inherited with the house. The agent's particulars had described it as a moated farmhouse, which was rather a play on words. Nevertheless, it was approached by an ancient brick-built bridge at the end of a long drive from the road, lined with poplar trees – hence its name. The whole place, with its willow edged ponds and mellowed buildings was a sort of Shangri La, but I was only there for three years before events beyond my control drove me, happily, as it has turned out, to South Wales.

My happiest memories of Suffolk are of ditch-crawling in my *Waterwitch* on the Blackwater, Stour, and Deben. She was a clinker-built gaff-rigged craft with red ochre sails and a heavy centreboard that took all my strength to winch up. I dared not let it down very far in those muddy tidal waters, where I could only get in and out of my anchorage for about an hour on either side of the top of the tide.

In those happy far off days, all one had to do at Manningtree to get a mooring was to dig a hole in the mud at low tide and sink a lorry wheel with a chain attached to a buoy. There were only a few boats there anyway, most of which belonged to local fishermen and retired bargemen. For it was from Manningtree and Mistley that the crews of the great yachts like Lipton's *Shamrock* were recruited, and the annual barge races on the Blackwater were a sight to behold.

At Mistley in those days – I hope they are still there now – there were huge flocks of swans, attracted there by the maltings, and I shall never forget early mornings floating down the river with just enough wind to have steerage way, and sailing right through the middle of them. They never seemed to mind; I expect they regarded my boat and I as part of kindly nature, like themselves.

And then there was that never to be forgotten day in the early 1960s when I was sailing alone in the lower reaches of the Stour on my way to the Walton on the Nazebacks. I noticed an oddly familiar tanker at anchor in the river, no doubt laid up there and awaiting a voyage to the scrapyard.

I steered closer, and yes, there was the name painted on the stern, the *Nacella*, on which I had sailed as Chief Radio Officer over twenty years previously. She was owned by the Anglo-Saxon Petroleum Company, later to be known as Shell, and in 1943 I made two crossings of the Atlantic on her. The battle of the Atlantic had by then seen the U-boat attacks very much less successful, but there were still enough sinkings to make life uncomfortable. Looking at my discharge book, I see that her tonnage was 7,149 tons, and what is interesting today is that she carried the Commodore Master of the fleet, and a crew of at least sixty. In 1982, during my second period at sea, I was the Radio Officer of a 300,000-ton tanker which could have comfortably accommodated the *Nacella* on its fore-deck. It carried a crew of 28, and had an unmanned engine room with a Chief and three engineer officers, who as far as I could see only occasionally went down to the engine control room to check that nothing was showing up on the warning systems, and these rang in the engineers' cabins anyway.

The officers, of whom there were nine (including myself), apart from their watches, spent their time exercising on deck, doing gigantic wooden crossword puzzles six feet by four, and in the evenings playing cards or watching films. They were Basques, fascinating and charming people, who, like friends I have in southern Ireland, had learned the secret of 'taking life aisy'. At eleven o'clock every morning all the officers who were not actually on watch, and this in practice meant one deck officer on the bridge, would adjourn to the 'tapas' room, which was a large area allocated specially for the purpose, where a long table was loaded with canape-type snacks and caraffes of red and white wine. This was followed one and a half hours later by lunch in the officer's saloon.

How different it all was to the Texaco super-tanker on which I had previously served, which carried double the number of crew, including fourteen engineers, and virtually limped from port because the engines kept breaking down. It had been built to do sixteen knots, but never went more than ten in case the vessel shook to pieces and foundered.

The *Nacella* had a companion gangway down the side and I would have liked to tie up *Waterwitch* and go aboard. But it was too risky. I was on my own and there was a strong tide running, so I sailed on, watching the *Nacella* and a piece of my past fade into the distance. I suppose she was awaiting her last voyage to the breaker's yard, for there were many such anchored in the lower Stour in those days, overtaken by events, with silent cabins and a deserted bridge.

Chapter 9

COWS AND MUCK-HEAPS
– TWO YEARS' HARD LABOUR

AT THE END OF 1971 I was the Personnel and Operating Manager of the Marconi Marine Company, and acutely conscious that my star was waning rapidly. It is a characteristic hazard besetting that pitiable creature, 'The Senior Executive', that as he approaches Nirvana in the shape of the General Manager's chair he either reaches it or becomes sidelined. Sidelining was obviously in the wings, so instead of clinging for several years like a barnacle on a tide-washed rock I resigned and purchased the little dairy farm of Coynant at Llanfynydd, roughly halfway between Llandeilo and Carmarthen. This insanity had been prompted by the headline 'Carmarthen – Land of Milk and Money' on the front page of a copy of the *Farmer's Weekly* that had somehow entered my field of vision. My only previous acquaintance with cows had been to avoid them in a field, so that it was with a mixture of apprehension and acute awareness of my folly that I found myself in the brucellosis-free cattle market at Carmarthen, where I purchased at auction seventeen Friesian cows or 'black and whites' as the natives call them.

My sole ideas about dairy farming were derived from books and the James Herriot films on television, and both turned out to be misleading. In fact the most useful book was William Cobbett's *Cottage Economy*, circa 1830. Far from dragging calves out with ropes under lantern light I would put the expectant mother in a comfortable barn with plenty of hay, and the next morning she would be there, contentedly licking her offspring. I never lost a single calf, but hated the distasteful task of immediately taking it away from the mother. She was then milked, and the result – a thick yellowy substance rather like thin custard and full of good things, fed to the calf.

Nowadays, I am sickened when I see what man does to his fellow inhabitants of the planet. Dairy milk as it is produced today is not a natural substance; nature decreed about a gallon, not the six or even eight gallons the unfortunate beasts have to stagger into the dairy with. Even worse was the barren market where worn out milkers are sold for butchers' meat. A dairy cow, along with that Queen of Spain, can bitterly complain: 'It's a hell of a game, three minutes pleasure and nine months pain, three months off and at it again.' Cows are described as 'two-calvers, three-calvers', and so on, and certainly after seven wind up being prodded with sticks into the barren market.

Even worse are the fate of sheep. I never see a field of sheep grazing in the beautiful Welsh hills without thinking of the horrible fate awaiting them, crowded into lorries and taken as far as the Middle East, where their throats are cut and their blood drained away as part of the ceremonies of 'religion'.

Running a small hillside dairy farm on one's own is little more than physical slavery. A visiting friend once pointed to my neighbour, bowed and tanned by the elements, remarking how agile he appeared for an old man. Actually, he was only in his early forties, and looked as though he had been beaten over the head with a plank.

The economics of the small one-man-band farm are tied up in getting in the hay. During the summer the cows 'get the milk off the grass', but in the winter they are tied up in the cowshed, and have to be fed with a mixture of that and bought-in feed.

When the hay is cut, it has to be 'tedded' which involves towing a rake-like contraption over it which fluffs it all about and allows the air to get in amongst it. Next it is dragged into long rows where it is picked up by a binding machine and punched into oblong parcels which the machine 'binds' with baler twine. The bales then have to be stored in a barn, where there is always the danger of fire due to internal combustion. The great key is not to cut your grass when it is likely to be ruined by rain, and in this I was very successful, which, in view of my inexperience, impressed my neighbours, who didn't seem to realise that I just waited until they cut theirs.

Next comes the nightmare of milking, which has to be done twice a day, and cows have never heard of Christmas Day or Sundays. The milk is extracted by clamping vacuum suckers on the bladder teats connected to special containers. It then has to be cooled and poured into churns, which are then labelled with the name of your farm, put on a trailer and towed down to a platform outside the farm gate, where they were collected by the Milk Marketing Board lorry. In the summer there was always the danger that the churns would become heated and the milk spoiled. Of course, nowadays, with herds of perhaps hundreds of cows, it is all piped straight in the milk lorries. I soon found that the Marketing Board had the finances tied up to suit them; in the summer when the milk came off the grass they paid less, and it was carefully adjusted to give the farmer enough to make his operation just viable.

The process of milking was fraught with danger; a cow can easily kill you if it kicks your head while you are bending down to clamp on the milking suckers. In any case some cows kick about so that the suckers fall off and get covered with a mixture of cow dung and straw. Here my old friend William Cobbett came to my rescue, because somewhere he had written that a cow does not like its tail pulled vertically upwards. With bad offenders I would put a bight in the end of a rope and after lassooing the cow's tail, throw it over a beam and haul it bar tight. If the cow kicked its legs came off the ground. Sometimes I would beat the cow with a stick, and then put my arms around its neck and apologise, explaining that I simply had to get the milk out somehow. And in the end a miracle happened – the cows seemed to understand, and they all became rather like pets, which made me feel even worse, realising their eventual fate.

After two years of this nightmarish existence, I sold all my cows to a man who had lost his herd through brucellosis for twice what I had paid for them. In the end I sold the farm, together with another small adjoining one I had purchased for about four times what I had paid for them in the first place, and I went back to sea to earn enough money to pay off the capital gains tax.

My chief memory is the kindness of my Welsh neighbours and it is nice to have this opportunity of recording it.

Chapter 10

THE WONDERFUL SEA CHARMED ME FROM THE FIRST

Joshua Slocum (*Sailing Alone Round the World*)

I FORGET HOW MANY TIMES I have sailed around the world with Captain Joshua Slocum in his yawl, *Spray*, which he rebuilt plank by plank at Fairhaven in 1892/3. Fairhaven is opposite New Bedford in the USA, long the home of whaling ship captains in the days of Moby Dick, and as he was re-building her it was under the scrutiny, and benefited from the advice of the retired old whaling captains, who 'worked up along' to view his progress. And when he set up the new stem-post they came from far and wide to see it, and with one voice pronounced it 'fit to smash ice'.

Joshua Slocum, Joseph Conrad, and my other hero, the Victorian explorer Sir Richard Burton, have been the beacons of my life, and like them a large part of it has been spent in continuous – perhaps I should call it restless – travel around the globe. Sometimes, as with Sir Richard Burton, it has provided a means of escape, and the urge still remains, though I believe its origin springs from a desire for excitement which I should by now have grown out of. But I fear it never will. I once read somewhere that adventures tend to happen to the adventurous, and I can still never resist placing myself in fortune's path if the chance arises. How undignified, in my mid-seventies!

Elsewhere in this book I have been unable to avoid mentioning my time at sea, and a whole chapter, if not restricted to morsels that might be interesting, might bore the reader to distraction. So I approach it with extreme caution.

When I went to sea in 1942, by one of the extraordinary operations of fate that thread my life like a string of beads, I joined my first ship, the *Ocean Viscount* in Swansea, within a quarter of a mile of where I now live. She was a standard wartime vessel built on the west coast of the USA, and in her I made two voyages to North Africa, carrying supplies for the Eighth Army. As I have related in chapter seven, I was next sent to the *Lorca* as Chief Radio Officer at a ridiculously young age, and after a voyage to West Africa joined another old ship of similar vintage.

My next ship was the *Baxtergate*, owned by Turnbull Scott of West Hartlepool, and is worth more than a passing mention, because she too was a period piece. She had about her that unique ambience which only comes when you combine the smell of live steam, salt spray, and brine-soaked hemp rope with an old ship that has tramped the oceans of the world for a quarter of a century and has an atmosphere aboard it somehow redolent of those who sailed in her and the ports she has visited. The *Baxtergate* was a partial example of what was called a 'blister' ship – when a profile of a cross-section of the hull takes the shape of two bulges running fore and aft along the length of the vessel. It was an idea generated in the 1920s for saving money on Suez Canal dues, where the levy was based on the width of the ship at deck level. It was only a short term success, for it did not take the Canal authorities long to solve the problem; they just amended the rules. And anyway the bulges inside the holds complicated cargo stowage.

Since West Hartlepool has cropped up, I cannot resist the temptation of repeating the famous story of how during the Napoleonic wars a monkey managed to swim ashore there from a French shipwreck, and was mistaken by the locals for a French spy and promptly hung. There is, however, a recent corollary, because it is said that the crew of an American space craft returning to earth included a monkey, and while they were discussing where they might land, someone asked the monkey where he thought it might be. The monkey, who was eating a banana at the time replied: 'I couldn't give a f...k, as long as it's not West Hartlepool!'

The *Baxtergate* was very much a definite survivor. In 1941, before I joined her, she was one of nine ships which sailed independently from Capetown to join a homeward bound convoy at Freetown, Sierra Leone, and after five anxious days she was the only one to survive the U-boats.

She was originally the s.s. *Anglo-Indian*, built in 1925 by Short Brothers of Sunderland for £50,000 for the Nitrate Producer Steamship Company, and bought and re-named by Turnbulls in 1937.

I have fond memories of the old *Baxtergate*. She had a vintage wireless room filled with equipment which would grace the present Marconi Museum in Chelmsford, and a long saloon table lined with circular rotating chairs bolted to the deck. I remember the Chief Engineer had false teeth which were hinged and sprung, like rich Uncle Fred, a character in the *Beano*, and on occasion would fly out of his mouth when he laughed or coughed. At meal times he would take them out and place them by the side of his plate when sitting down to eat. He once solemnly asked me if I knew the smallest engineering measurement known to man, and when I shook my head explained that it was 'a nick on a gnat's nut'.

The officers' cabins were lined with white painted wooden match-boarding, and every evening in mine an army of cockroaches, or jaspers, as we used to call them, would come out and march in stately columns in search of food. It was the practice for each of the officers to have a supper placed in his cabin in the form of a mug with cocoa and a spoonful of condensed milk – connie-onnie – and a doorstep cheese or corned beef sandwich. The only way I could keep jaspers out of my supper was to suspend the mug by string from the deck-head, where it performed as a plumb-bob with the rolling and pitching of the ship. Even then the jaspers marched down the string and filled the bottom, from where I would pick them out before going down to the galley to add hot water. It still tasted excellent, and I suppose the moral is – such things are all in the mind.

We went down to North Africa, again with tanks and ammunition, and at that time of course the ships sailed in convoy, at a speed dictated by the slowest ship, which was usually seven and a half knots. This meant that the bridge officer had to maintain a set distance from the ship in the column ahead, and he did this by ringing down to the engine room and saying 'two up' or 'two down', meaning the engine revolutions. I was on watch one dark night – I did the eight to twelve – when the Captain rang down from the bridge with the urgent message: 'Sparks, come up the bridge and bring your screw-drivers.' I rushed up to find him standing by the binnacle, and by its dim light I could make out the quarter-master, who should have been at the ship's wheel, retrieving it from where it had rolled to the wing of the wheelhouse. The ship was heading straight for the adjoining column of ships, and it was a nasty moment, until we managed to get the wheel back in place just in time to avoid disaster.

In after years, Captain Ellis, an Ulsterman, retired to Cardiff, where a few years before he died I had the pleasure of meeting him again, and many a laugh did we have over the old *Baxtergate*.

We discharged our cargo at Algiers, and then went down to Casablanca to pick up manganese ore for home. My chief memory of the place is that it was teeming with newly-landed American soldiers destined for the big push to Cairo. A minor mystery to us was how so many of them, clearly recent conscripts, displayed several medals. I must be wrong, but I believe one medal was awarded for joining the army and a second for having landed safely at Casablanca! In spite of this they were a jolly crowd, who packed the nightspots, and distributed chewing-gum to Arab children.

The only other memory worth mentioning concerns a nightclub I visited there with some friends from the ship, where I encountered an unique example of the Arab genius for extracting baksheesh. The toilet I used had no handle on the inside of the door, which had to be closed and locked from the outside by a gracious Moroccan personality who ushered me in with a beaming smile. To get out one banged on the door, to be greeted with an open palm and a notification of the minimum charge, authorised by the management, who presumably subcontracted this valuable concession.

The *Welsh Troubador*, owned by Gibbs of Newport, Mon., was rather special because of her association with Wales. She was a general purpose bulk carrier, one of four similar ships owned by the company. Once, while we were coming out of Alexandria, three of the fleet, including ourselves, were there at the same time, a fact not of general interest now but a source of great satisfaction to us at the time, as we sailed past the other two as they lay at anchor on our way out.

My time on her is best summed up by saying that we tramped around the world for sixteen months, never visiting the same place twice, and sometimes drifting for days in mid-ocean while the owners were fixing another cargo on the Baltic Exchange. It was a peculiar experience when the owners told us 'to go and lose ourselves for a few days' until they radioed our next orders, which could have literally been anywhere. During that time everybody on board felt unsettled, especially if the engines were stopped, and the usual shipboard sounds and motion ceased. We felt we were in an unpleasant limbo, and everyone breathed a sigh of relief when we got going again. For our Captain it could be a strain, as for example when we were ordered to loiter about in the Gulf of Akaba, a relatively narrow waterway where the ship couldn't anchor, and had to keep steaming up and down, keeping out of the way of other ships.

Akaba itself was an unusual port for water was too deep to anchor, and ships tied up beween a bow rope from the shore and a buoy astern. Eventually, we went to Amman ourselves and tied up in this manner, while the cargo was handled by lighters.

Just opposite to Amman, in a distance best measured in yards, lay the Israeli port of Elat, which in marked contrast to sleepy Amman, presented each evening a waterfront spectacle of car headlights and the neon signs of nightspots, like a miniature Times

Square. It was the prime holiday resort of Israel, heaving with bars and all the delights of a night on the town. This night-spotters paradise, so near to Amman, was separated from Jordan by a heavily guarded border generated by the Jewish/Arab troubles of the time.

The British captain of the ship tied up next to us learned that, having a British passport, he would be waved through the border to sample the night life on Elat. In fact he could just walk there. What nobody had told him was that he couldn't get back, so when his evening out had ended, he found himself stranded in Israel, and unable to return to his ship. In the end he had to fly to London, obtain a new passport, because his existing one had been franked in Elat, which would have precluded admission to Jordan. He eventually returned to his ship several days later after a very expensive night out.

Our genial captain, Phillip Baxter, to whom, if these words should ever enter his field of vision, I send my cordial regards, and hope he will be able to handle my change of name, made our voyage a happy one with his combination of good discipline and relaxed congeniality, and it was with great regret that sixteen months later I left his ship in Marseilles.

It was on the *Welsh Troubador* that by a happy mischance I quitted the unsavoury habit of smoking. It was my practice to roll my own cigarettes in brown liquorice paper; I probably felt that it gave me the air of the sort of Russian émigré who haunted the south of France in the stories of Somerset Maugham, and drank tea out of a glass. (I am glad to say that I have never drunk tea out of a glass myself.)

I joined in Liverpool, where ahead of us lay the long passage to New Zealand and I took with me a large supply of liquorice brown cigarette papers. In fact, I took several boxes of packets. But when I came to use them they were all stuck together, and expanded into long concertinas as I opened each packet. I then discovered that I could not smoke a roll-up without them, and by the time we reached Dunedin I no longer needed a cigarette, and while it took me three months to stop coughing, I have rid myself of the habit since that day.

Signing off in Marseilles I became introduced to the magic of French railway travel. I had a lot of baggage, accumulated over the lengthy time I had been on the ship, and was deposited with it by the agent, just before midnight, to catch a train that had started off in Cannes. I had kindly been provided with a first-class sleeper to Paris, and was looking forward to a comfortable journey. The platform was little more than a long, badly lit stretch of concrete about a foot below the steps of the train, which arrived an hour late. It was crowded with people, including North Africans with mountains of belongings, and the train was already packed, with standing room in the corridors only. Somehow in the mad rush, for the train only stopped at the station for a few minutes, I managed to squeeze into the corridor, rammed in by the people behind.

And there I stood, like an upright sardine, with no prospect of moving up the train to get to my empty 1st class sleeper, all the way to Paris. At one point the ticket collector shoved his way along the corridor, and I explained my predicament to him, whereupon he rolled his eyes and shrugged his shoulders with that Gallic indifference I envy so much. It is the French secret weapon, and serves them so well in ignoring all the common market regulations which they find inconvenient but ensure that everybody else complies with. *Vive La France!* Would that we might follow their glorious example.

On my return to sea after twenty-six years ashore, my second voyage on the *Corabank* reigns supreme. She was a general purpose cargo vessel, built specially for the Bank Line, who tramped all over the world, but were mainly famous for their connections in the South Pacific, where they also had extensive interests in the Islands. My first voyage on the *Corabank*, the first of her class, was a good example of the fantastic run she had been designed for. After loading a general cargo in the UK and Rotterdam we sailed for New Orleans, where we lay alongside in the heart of the French Quarter for nearly three glorious weeks while the ship discharged and loaded another general cargo for the Islands and Australasia. I was able to soak myself in New Orleans jazz, the dizzy charms of Bourbon Street, and Old Big Muddy, with its Levees and stern-wheelers with a steam organ grinding out all my favourite music on the top deck; one of my favourite places on earth. I even managed to get up to Baton Rouge, capital of Louisanna, and home of the celebrated crooked Governor Huey Long between the wars.

He was the Al Capone of the South, though not quite so obviously bloodstained. A huge statue of him stands in Baton Rouge near the State Building, and locally his name is revered. They will tell you that it was Huey Long who built the schools, established hospitals, and free libraries. He used to live in a large mansion, rather like something from the set of 'Gone With the Wind', which lay at the end of a long avenue among the cotton fields. Many sensible citizens would drop by and without presuming to bother Huey personally, leave presents of one kind of another, more or less on the porch. It was said that Huey, when once asked about this, laughed and commented, 'Well, I like all this stuff!'

Then it was through the Panama canal calling at Samoa, Fiji, Noumea, and various small islands where we picked up copra and importantly, palm oil, for which the *Corabank* was fitted with specially heated tanks. The islands, especially the small ones, were extraordinary places, for they were so unspoilt – at least they were thirty years ago. The expatriates who worked there, mostly British, Australian or Hong Kong Chinese, lived a relaxed life. Many were refugees from urban Australia and qualified for the term, 'Island Happy', a description more an envious one than critical. Most worked hard in the forestry and their own businesses, and played even harder in the clubs, with their well-equipped bars and social activities, in perpetual sunshine.

And days steaming across the Pacific, in fantastic weather, with weekend barbecues on deck and parties around the swimming pool, are memories that will live with me for ever.

I had a Nancy Sinatra tape which included 'These boots are made for walking', and I only have to play it to bring back those golden days.

Then followed Burnie, Tasmania, Melbourne, Sydney, Townsville, New Guinea, and back through the Red Sea. Everywhere it was several days in port, for those were the happy times when ships still had derricks and twenty-four hour turn-rounds were unheard of.

The Captain was Spen Lynch, to whom I send greetings, should these lines ever come before him. I wonder if he remembers how we climbed up the radar mast on top of the bridge and brought down the twelve foot radar scanner so that I could repair it? There was a twenty knot wind blowing at the time and the ship was doing seventeen knots, and we had to rope the scanner to prevent it from blowing away.

By another glorious twist of fate, nine years later, on almost my last trip to sea, I joined the *Corabank* again, for more or less the same voyage. It was the end of an era, for by then the Bank Line, with the rest of British shipping, was winding down, and soon it had all vanished, just a memory for people like myself and Spen Lynch.

Chapter 11

THE SMILE ON THE FACE OF GIACONDA

The Labyrinth of Gender

It is occasionally argued that, excepting for the fundamental relation of the female to a child to whom she has given birth, our remaining social behaviour can be largely traced to parental indoctrination. Little boys play with footballs and guns; little girls play with dolls and are encouraged to cook and take an interest in clothes. If these influences are reversed, the consequences are taken to be obvious.

But it is surely wrong to assume they lead automatically to the reality of transsexualism. It is far more likely that their consequences lodge within the brain in the form of neuronal connections, and contributes towards a state of mental androgony which I believe exists in every individual to a varying degree. I suspect that this lies at the root of ordinary interaction between the sexes; and only rarely does it emerge externally as transsexualism. However, this is only part of the story, for undoubtedly most individuals who have crossed the gender divide have been conscious of a gender problem from their earliest recollections.

If one has to sum it up, it takes the form of an overwhelming feeling that one is presenting one's self externally to the world in the wrong gender. In my own case it did not emerge in a traditional form, in that my interests never included wanting to play with dolls or learn to sew or cook. My favourite toys were building bricks, Meccano, pedal cars, sailing model yachts, and taking pot shots with airguns.

The story is told of Lord Castlereagh, 2nd Marquess of Londonderry, that his recipe for dealing with problems was to confront them head-on. The success of this was vividly illustrated when he encountered a malignant and threatening apparition in his bedroom. He advanced boldly towards the spectre, whereupon it promptly fell back in confusion and vanished. When the time came that circumstances permitted me to follow Lord Castlereagh's example and confront my difficulty, my own problems disappeared like a ghost at cock-crow.

The only comment I have to add to those experiencing a similar difficulty, which I make with great reluctance, is that such an escape is only practicable if at the end of the day the illusion (for that it what it is), is acceptable to the outside world. Failing this, the second state can only be worse.

Since, more than twenty years ago, I took the plunge, I have never experienced any difficulty in social contacts, and I have found women particularly supportive. Initially, there were a few exceptions, restricted to men not famous for brains or manners who lived in the same road, so that my change in lifestyle entered their field of vision somewhat dramatically. I had the feeling that not only did they regard it as somehow threatening the sacred rights of masculinity, but as possibly contagious. I had a distinct sense of lumpen male libidos beginning to wobble.

A sense of unease and dissatisfaction with the gender role under which I was required to operate is one of my earliest recollections, and at first it was intertwined with a desperate hope that somehow, if I tried hard enough, a miracle would occur to sort it out. But that never happened, and it came to reside in the back of my mind as a shameful secret I could never share with anyone else. And then on one shattering day in 1933 even that minor comfort was taken from me when I was travelling out with my parents to Naples on the Orient Liner *Orama*.

As usual I was endeavouring to avoid playing with the other children on board, while at the same time envying them the good time they were having. Then one of them, a pleasant boy of about my own age, came up to me and said, very politely: 'I say, are you a boy or a girl?' Looking back, I expect it was probably just due to my mother's penchant for dressing me in floppy hats and tunics, with button-up shoes. But my embarrassment and humiliation seemed to extend to the horizon, and thereafter my insecurity reached epic proportions.

Eventually, I was sent away to school, where to my relief I encountered no such problems; there were others of a different kind. Having been educated more or less entirely at home until the age of ten I was light years ahead in everything except languages, mathematics and religion. When it was discovered that I was unacquainted with the Lord's Prayer, I was made to stand in front of the class and held up to ridicule as a pagan.

On the positive side there have been gratifying occasions, which have steadily become more frequent as the circle of my acquaintances has grown following the publication of my various books, when I have had to introduce the subject myself. These situations usually arise when a casual remark of mine might puzzle the listener. For instance, if in the course of conversation, I have occasion to remark that I went to sea as a Radio Officer in the Merchant Navy in 1942, an expression ranging from perplexity to dark suspicion is likely to appear on the countenance of the other party. Am I a romancer, or a liar? Then, as a penalty for not editing my remarks, I have to drop the bombshell. And now I have reached the point where I no longer edit my conversation to avoid such situations. To tell the truth, they entertain me, and I rather enjoy them.

The saying that each individual is an island is never truer than when applied to sex. One can never really know what goes on in another's mind, even between people who have lived together for years. And sometimes I wonder if then it may not be even worse. Strange fantasies and desires can lurk within the human psyche, sometimes with corroding results.

It is not so many years ago that readers of the tabloid press were entertained by the story of the proprietress of a certain bawdy house, lavishly equipped with a variety of torture chambers and weapons of flagellation ranging from cat-o'-nine-tails to slabs of wet fish, who successfully evaded the clutches of the Inland Revenue by crossing the Atlantic with her business diary, a copy of which she had probably lodged with a third party as life insurance. It may be no more than a scurrilous rumour, but the list was said to embrace a large cross-section of what are jokingly described as the higher levels of society. Members of the aristocracy, Church of England, Legislators from both Houses, Captains of Industry, and a sprinkling of public schoolmasters, were said to be well represented, and it is believed that the lady still derives a comfortable pension from many sources.

The days when a change of gender attracted wide attention – and an individual whose only claim to public interest it was could sell the story for a lot of money – have long since vanished. Nowadays, individuals who successfully make the transition quietly merge into society and get on with their lives, as I have been fortunate enough to be able to do. There is little doubt that when people encounter the reality of a gender change they are usually intrigued. Speaking for myself it has turned to be a large plus.

I believe that the answer to the perplexing question of gender confusion lies deeply rooted in the phenomonen of androgyny. By that I am referring to its mental and not its physical manifestation.

It is customary at the present time for certain fashionable psychiatrists to rubbish the work of Carl Jung, not least by dwelling, with a sly titter, on certain aspects of his private life, as if his seminal work on the anima and animus did not tower above those who denigrate him. They are like those citizens of Chartres, who wanted to tear down the cathedral because it dominated too offensively their foolish little city. It is in the opposing effects of the anima and animus within the human psyche that the answer to the problem can be discovered, and it is not obscure or unnatural. Indeed, I would argue that it is not only natural, but in no way surprising, and has been built into the system by the mysterious Mind that is responsible for the creation of life on Earth.

The interplay between the qualities of the anima and the animus creates a whole series of permutations which revolve around the central orbit of androgyny. It is perfectly possible for a very masculine individual with a voice like Bluto to have a strongly developed feminine side to his mind. And the reverse equally applies, so that within a partnership a range of behaviour and drives can exist between two extremes on either side of a cusp where both are balanced and one compliments the other. When this occurs, either within a partnership or an individual, it is not unreasonable to suggest that a superior relationship or personality will result. That this is true is borne out by a moment's reflection on the number of individuals throughout history – Rulers, Generals, Philosophers, Writers, Artists, Sculptors, Inventors – who we know were sexually ambivalent and whose lives and creativity speak for themselves.

It is interesting to try and sum up the predominate atavistic qualities of the anima and animus, which so often act in opposition:

Feminine

1. The natural influences which arise from bearing children.
2. An ability to bear greater pain.
3. A more highly developed sense of human sympathy.
4. Controversially, recent school and training reports suggest that women not only possess a higher ability to absorb information, but also the ability to put it into practice in such varied fields as Medicine, flying Jumbo-Jets, Fighter Aircraft, Commanding Deep-Sea Ships, the Stock Exchange, top Television reporting, and War Correspondents. And these are of course in addition to the traditional female occupations of teaching and nursing, and do not include the arts.
5. The application of judgement by instinct.

Male

1. Aggression.
2. A tendency to take refuge in the role of 'Man the Mighty Hunter', who protects and provides for his women folk and children.
3. Frequently, a feeling of being threatened by women whose achievements extend beyond domestic chores and such traditional activities as teaching or nursing.
4. Sometimes secret fears of sexual inadequacy. It is much easier for a woman to hide these when they exist.

When all these ingredients are stirred up in a pot in varying quantities, and brought to the boil in the course of ordinary human interaction and the stresses and strains of life, the complexity of the situation is obvious. But in the middle of this vortex of emotions lies an area of stability, like in the eye of a hurricane, where the forces are equally balanced; and calm prevails, the hedonistic state of androgyny.

This is how I describe my own condition, at least to myself, in spite of the fact that my passport clearly states 'Joanna Greenlaw. Sex: Female'. Cosmetic surgery, however externally convincing, does not alter the fact that an individual born male possesses a prostate gland. The reality is that I am an androgynous individual living very happily as a woman.

The present era of patriarchal subjugation of women in Europe and the Middle East seems only to have commenced as late as around 3,000 BC. This coincides roughly with the overthrow of the Minoan civilisation on Crete by the Myceneans, which, contrary to that arch patriarchal interpreter of archaeology, Sir Arthur Evans, was dedicated to the High Priestess.

It reached its peak in the Judeo/Christian, and later Muslim, eras, based on the convenient myth of humankind's downfall into original sin following Eve's infamous temptation of Adam with her celebrated apple. From that moment Man, the Mighty Hunter, moved on to the high moral ground and women were relegated to bearing children, domestic chores, fetching water from the well, or labouring in the fields, while the men sat around talking. The era of andro-centric thinking had begun, just as pre-Copernican thinking was geocentric.

Before this phantasmagoria descended on the world, a very different order prevailed; for it was that of the Earth Mother, whose figures, statues, and temples are to be found all over Europe and the Middle East, and beyond.

She had been worshipped from the beginning of the Neolithic period, circa 7,000 BC, and some authorities put it as far back as the Upper Paleolithic Age at circa 25.000 BC. The Fall of Humankind occasioned by the scandalous behaviour of that insidious Jade Eve is by comparison, as of yesterday; it comes in at about 1,600 BC. The overwhelming evidence of the Original Earth Mother worship has been successfully buried and obfuscated by the sexual and religious bias of generations of male scholars. Nearly all the archaeologists, historians and theologians of the 19th and 20th centuries were brought up within societies dominated by the male-orientated religions of Judaism, Christianity, or Islam, and it is only recently that the pendulum is beginning to swing back.

In considering the reason for the existence of these primeval drives within the human psyche, one comes to a fork in the road to enlightenment; is human life the result of a cosmic accident as protagonists of the Big Bang inform us? Or is a Universal Mind at work? Here I must reveal myself in my true colours. I believe that the Big Bang theory is as suspect as the doom-laden warnings of the global warming prophets.

One cannot postulate a Big Bang without first explaining where its ingredients came from. In the ancient world it was believed that the Earth was supported on the back of a tortoise, and no one raised the awkward question of the absence of the Emperor's clothes by asking what the tortoise stood on. Nor for that matter, do the Big Bang merchants today.

Sir James Jeans wrote in the late 1920s that, in his opinion, the Universe was not only queer, but queerer than we can ever suppose. If human intelligence is not the result of a chemical accident then it must have been produced by some Universal Force. Could it be that elsewhere in the Universe there might be other life which we could recognise, that might even be androgynous and not require two sexes to reproduce itself? And could some infinitesimal trace of such a cosmic ancestor lie hidden within the deepest recesses of our psyche, perhaps brought to Earth as a gene riding on a meteorite?

My secret predicament, for so it remained until my middle forties, might well have remained bottled up forever, and I might never have had peace of mind and a freedom from guilty conscience had not an incident in my life about that time not blown everything wide apart, and I felt I might as well be hung for a sheep as a lamb. The details concern no one but myself and those involved, and old hurts are best left buried in the past, where they belong.

Reflecting on these events thirty years later, I now recognise an inevitability about them I did not see at the time. If a moral can be extracted, it is that difficulties not confronted just fester and grow. What appeared then as a disaster I now see as the kindly operation of fate, for when the moment arrived that my responsibilities allowed me to take decisive action, I discovered that the walls which restrain us so often exist only in our imagination and vanish at the touch of a firm hand.

In the mid '60s, the UK press was suddenly filled with the dramatic story of a woman racing driver called Roberta Cowell, who had translated herself from a Battle of Britain Spitfire pilot into the sort of gorgeous blonde every man wants to marry. Not long afterwards she was followed by April Ashley, who had followed a similar path; and after visiting a sex-change clinic in Casablanca with a suitcase full of used American dollars, married the Hon. Arthur Corbett, the son of Lord Rowallan.

Then followed a spectacular divorce, when the English Establishment closed ranks, and declared that a transsexual could have no married rights under the law, and the marriage, which had taken place in Gibraltar, was classified as illegal.

These juicy details filled the papers at the time, but for me it was a watershed, because I realised, looking at these glamorous creatures, that given a good start from Mother Nature anyway (essential!) there was a way out of my secret predicament. I decided to dip my toe in the waters, and begin to venture into the twilight world of the transsexual.

This shadowy world largely centered on well-known drag pubs frequented by drag entertainers, transvestites, transsexuals – secret or otherwise – and a whole raft of curious spectators attracted, for various reasons, to the scene. It formed a sort of inter-connected network scattered over the metropolis, and each pub had its own following.

Things tended to reach a crescendo on weekends, and the most popular pubs, i.e. those with the best entertainers, would be filled to capacity shortly after opening. Extra customers trying to squeeze in would be discouraged by the management, often in terms that left no room for doubt.

I have not visited these scenes of an odd period in my life for thirty years, and am told that while the same scenes still exist, most of the old atmosphere has departed, replaced by modern stages and all the paraphernalia of rows of theatre seats and flashing lights. And with it has gone the genuine old East End pub ambience, along with Victorian cut-glass mirrors, polished mahogany bars, brass foot-rails and sawdust floors. Like the England of my youth, they have disappeared like the buffalo, never to return.

Perhaps, in case no-one else gets round to it, I should set down for posterity one good example, the old Vauxhall Tavern on the south side of the river, under the shadow of the immense iron Vauxhall Bridge.

It is Friday evening at about seven o'clock, and I have spent the day at meetings in London. Instead of catching the first train home at Liverpool Street, I have decided to catch the last, and pay a visit to the Vauxhall Tavern. Its existence was unknown to me until the previous month when I read an article in the *Queen* magazine about a pub drag entertainer called Bow who performed there. That was in the great days of the *Queen* magazine before it changed hands, when it was full of interesting, stimulating and controversial articles, and pictures of beautiful women, and soon to be taken over and ruined, like so much else which once possessed the elusive quality called style.

It was late Autumn, and cold outside, but in the pub the temperature must have been up in the nineties. It was already crowded with a glorious mixture of East End regulars, including a row of East End mums sitting along the back wall, gossiping and sipping glasses of stout and cracking jokes with acquaintances across the room, young men and their girlfriends, and a sprinkling of West End types who had ventured south of the river in search of a change of environment. The long polished U-shaped mahogany bar was a sea of glasses and spilt beer, with the barmen working flat out to meet orders, and the noise level was up in the paint cards.

The atmosphere was building up to a tense expectancy and rose to fever pitch when the barman shouted for last orders before the show began. Those completed, the top of the bar, which would form the stage, was mopped down, and a hush descended over the room. It was suddenly broken by a roll of drums, as an artist called Bow emerged, standing on the bar top, and proceeded to mime 'My Way' against the background of a record by Frank Sinatra, making her way around the bar as she did so. To deafening applause, a couple of other numbers followed, Bow moving up and down the bar somehow managing not to fall off, in spite of having to clutch onto a microphone lead. Edith Piaf's sob song 'No Regrets' wound up the performance, and Bow disappeared as quickly as she had come.

That was forty years ago, but I can still see her clearly, young, staggeringly beautiful in a low cut black dress, talented, and though I did not realise it at the time, tragic. I got to know her later on, and she once told me that she hated her work. Her ambition was to change sex properly and have a successful career on the stage, where I am sure she would have succeeded. But it was not to be. Years later I heard that Bow had been stabbed in the stomach and died on the way to hospital. I have never checked the story because I don't really want to know, but I have a horrible feeling that is how all that beauty, talent, vivacity, and love of life ended.

On the way out I overheard two attractive young women talking to each other about her.

'There's nobody as attractive as Bow,' I heard one say. 'She's got more sex appeal in her little finger than I have in my whole body.' Her companion giggled. 'I tell you what,' she said, 'My Old Man's out tonight, why don't you come round to my house; you can be the girl and I'll be the boy.'

Outside, it was pitch dark except for the street lamps, and the cold air and a sudden reaction made me shiver.

A group of winos had lit a small fire on a bombsite, and over their methylated spirits or cider, or whatever it was they were drinking, they were debating the mystery of the Universe, each one holding forth without listening to anybody else, like an Irish Parliament in full session.

In the street, as I made my way to the underground station beneath Vauxhall Bridge, I felt suddenly depressed as the world of make belief faded to reality in the cold and the dark. And at Liverpool Street Station I did not catch the train; instead, I stayed overnight at the Great Eastern Hotel and wrestled with a guilty conscience.

Chapter 12

PAMPAS, TANGOS, AND STEAKS WHICH OVERHUNG THE PLATE

Buenos Aires, 1946 and 1976

I FIRST WENT TO Buenos Aires on a ship called the *North Anglia*, owned by Hugh Roberts of Newcastle on Tyne. It was my second voyage on the ship; the first had been to Port Churchill, in the Hudson Bay, when the *North Anglia* was the first ship to visit Port Churchill after World War II.

Long a Hudson Bay fur trading post, Port Churchill had been developed during the 1930s as a convenient point to tranship grain from the American and Canadian middle-west, as a means of breaking the financial stranglehold imposed by business interests along the St Lawrence and Great Lakes. Several large grain elevators had been built there, which could be filled up over a period, and then emptied into ships during the few weeks the Hudson Bay was sufficiently free of ice to allow navigation.

My chief memory of Port Churchill is the annual trek of polar bears through the town, south in the winter, north in the summer, when they raided the bins, and sometimes broke into the pantries of the houses. I was told that if left alone they were not considered dangerous, being more interested in kitchen scraps than humans, but of course they were always a threat. I remember going for a walk around the harbour and being urgently advised by a local to get back to the ship as soon as possible, in case I encountered a bad tempered bear.

We took a cargo of grain back to Cardiff, and then sailed for Buenos Aires, steaming all the way at seven and a half knots, and calling at Cape Verde for bunkers. We arrived at Buenos Aires in the middle of a dock strike, so that we were alongside for a month before even beginning to discharge our cargo. When that was completed a fortnight later, we went up to the little iron ore port of San Nicolas, further up the River Plate, where we loaded for the UK.

I am writing this in September 2002 when apparently the economy of Argentina has collapsed, and even the middle and upper classes have been reduced to bartering in order to obtain their daily necessities. What happens when they have nothing left to sell is hard to contemplate. But when I arrived in Buenos Aires in 1946 it was still easy to see why, before the First World War, the city had been known as the Paris of the southern hemisphere. Wide tree-lined streets, gracious squares, public gardens, magnificent buildings, luxury shops filled to capacity, and everywhere the evidence of commercial prosperity, in spite of the recently ended war.

The Argentine economy was based on the immense beef ranches of the pampas, those vast grazing grounds which stretched into the interior of the country like a gigantic waveless green ocean. And the restaurants and bars! And for us merchant seamen there was but one order – steak and eggs. And what steaks! They overhung the plate and were surmounted by four fried eggs, sunny side up.

It was an economy which had been largely founded by British enterprise and capital. It was they who built the railways, ran the most important shipping agencies, and owned a large proportion of the vast beef estancias in the interior. From these came the export flood of beef carcasses and corned beef, mostly shipped to England through the port of Liverpool, and which drove the economy.

It was extraordinary, after seeing the wartime devastation of Europe to go ashore in Buenos Aires and find pre-war life apparently in full swing. The Harrods store there was an exact copy of the one in Knightsbridge. Except for the price labels in pesos, one might have been shopping in pre-war London.

In those happy, far-off days there was another mystery about Buenos Aires – every drink under the sun was available there – whisky, gin, vodka, liqueurs, all manufactured locally and on sale at half the UK price. They were all packaged in the familiar bottles, but if you looked closely the slightly smudgy printing gave the game away. But what did that matter to us – they tasted just as good and in the hot days of youth it was quantity more than quality that concerned us.

Along the bank of the River Plate, as it began to wind its long way up into the interior, and up to Rosario, there was a wide esplanade which extended for several miles until it merged into the docks, and eventually faded into the pampas. Every evening this was the scene of that typically Spanish ritual, the pre-evening meal stroll to see and be seen, especially for the young caballeros and senoritas.

Another surprising thing about Buenos Aires at that time were the number of vintage cars that were to be seen, many dating back to the 1920s, like a scene from a James Cagney gangster movie. I even once saw a Ford Model T. Thirty years later, when I went into Montevideo, across the river, on a ship called the *Ocean Transport*, owned by Houlders, I saw the same thing. They would have fetched a fortune in Europe, but at that time at any rate the government strictly forbade their export.

Then once again, fortune played one of her tricks on me, for that ship returned to Swansea, where I signed off and went to my home less than a mile away.

Eventually, we sailed for San Nicolas to load ore for home. It was then an unspoilt example of a little Argentinian town that was just about as Spanish as it was possible to be. Halfway up the River Plate to Rosario, Argentina's commercial gateway to the interior, it was situated on a cliff above the river, where there was room for one ship at a time to tie up below the shutes which poured ore into the holds.

The *North Anglia* was only a typical small steam tramp, basically of 1930s design, although built early in the war, but it still took five days to fill us up, which led to an unforgettable experience – a two-day drive into the interior of the pampas.

Captain Howard Kell, the Master of the *North Anglia*, had gone to sea between the wars, and the outbreak of war had found him Harbour Master of the little north-west coast port of Maryport. He went back to sea in 1940, and survived the war in spite of being torpedoed and sunk twice. Howard Kell was an efficient master, who ran a very happy yet well disciplined ship, but saw no reason why he should not leave his ship for a couple of days, safely tied up beneath the shutes at San Nicolas under the care of his chief officer.

The Radio Officer on a merchant ship operates in a little world of his own, responsible only to the master, amid his dots and dashes, weather reports, and ship's order. Depending on the Radio Officer, and the ship, and a particular master, it was sometimes possible for the latter to socialise with his Radio Officer to perhaps a greater extent than his navigating officers, though this was the reverse of being the usual situation. But Howard Kell seemed to like my conversation and he arranged with his very accommodating ship's agent (that was how such things were done in those relaxed days in up country Argentina) for the two of us to set off in a car for a couple of days, accompanied by two Spanish ladies with what might be best described as relaxed morals.

One was young and beautiful and about my own age, but she was allocated to Captain Kell. The other might have been an elder sister, a business associate, or even her mother, and she smiled at me with a mixture of motherly care and a terrifying hint of sexual adventures in store.

We spent a night at one of the scruffy little establishments, a cross between a lodging house and a taverna, that are dotted about the dreary waste of the pampas. Usually, these were surrounded by a few depressed looking dwellings, which form a community barely large enough to deserve a name. The customers are usually gauchos who work on the neighbouring haciendas, and the villagers themselves, whose relaxation seemed to boil down to drinking, playing cards, and strumming guitars, often very skilfully.

I managed, using sign language, to avoid the advances of the older lady, much to my own embarrassment and her annoyance, and escaped into a room of my own for the night, and instead shared my bed with various winged creatures which bit any exposed parts of my anatomy.

There is little to say about the pampas, except that it is dusty, flat, seemingly endless, infinitely boring, bounded only by the horizon, and the vast herds of cattle which it manages to support.

Thirty years later, when I returned to Buenos Aires on the *Ocean Transport*, it was a sad and depressing experience, for by then the country was already well into its slide to economic decline under the disastrous regime of President Peron and his consort, Eva. On the surface life still went on, but the shops were half empty, and everywhere were the signs of a once great city falling apart. The invariable indicators are always the decline of public services; nothing is repaired properly, and a general tattiness prevails.

One day I went to a gigantic flea market in the hope of picking up antiques at a favourable price. But I was sadly disillusioned. A large proportion of vendors seemed to be middle class people selling off, so to speak, their family silver. But there were no bargains, for London prices, almost to the pound, prevailed.

I was looking for something in the antiquarian horological line, or things like scientific instruments or musical boxes. I did find a magnificent turn-of-the-century Swiss musical box in mint condition, with a beautifully illustrated list of twenty-four tunes in the lid. The only problem was that it was £3,000, the going price in London.

Most depressing of all was seeing cultivated and intelligent people – they all spoke good English – reduced to such straits.

The past magnificence of the buildings added to the sense of desolation. The streets were dirty and the pavements in need of repair. Only the steak restaurants and drinks seemed to have survived, at least for foreigners with money in their pockets.

Police corruption was everywhere. If you returned to the ship with something legitimately purchased ashore the policeman at the gate would not allow you through without being bribed with cigarettes. One of these characters accompanied me back to the ship, much to the consternation of the captain, who thought I had been getting into trouble. But all the man wanted was a carton of two hundred cigarettes, which he demanded quite blatantly.

Sometimes in moments of philosophic social depression, I think I can understand the frame of mind of a Romanised landowner, say in south-west Gaul, perhaps in some pocket overlooked by the Gothic invaders, or even having established a kind of tolerance from them. Some such fortunate individual, living quietly among his vineyards and peasantry, would have realised the inevitability of the changes he was beginning to see all around him, and of the forthcoming collapse of his society and standards, not dissimilar to the times in which we now live.

Chapter 13

CLOCKS, SHIPS, AND WRITING

'Well, Mr Gibbon, still scribble, scribble, scribble?'
(William IV, on meeting Edward Gibbon)

It was not until I left the sea in 1984 that I could concern myself with matters other than the hurly burly of making a living, and meeting family responsibilities. By then I had decided to finally confront the secret gender problem which complicated my life for so many years. Until that was dealt with I could not concentrate on things which I considered important and which interested me. I have covered that problem elsewhere in this book, and the logistics and trauma of the process I choose to pass over, as boring to me, and of no interest to anyone else.

Originally, I felt that to be complete an autobiography should perhaps touch upon the author's mind as well as a life journey, and wrote a final chapter accordingly. But it emerged as a maelstrom of scientific, metaphysical and philosophical speculation, which I felt was best avoided so I destroyed it all, except for the last paragraph, in which I tried to sum up how far, if at all, I had progressed along the shadowy road to enlightenment. It appears at the end of this book, and speaks for itself.

I have always been fascinated by time, that commodity of which we have so little at our disposal. The Newtonian concept of absolute time, and the ideas of the determinists have now crumbled away, first under the onslaught of Einstein, Quantum physics, and the recognition of Chaos in particle physics, which I find immensely comforting.

On ships, where I have spent so much of my life, time regulates one's existence: watch-keeping periods, sleeping, and navigation. Or at least it did before the advent of satellites rendered daily sextant observations using a chronometer superfluous. It also generated in me an understanding of the shallow depths of the metric system, for life on our planet revolves around the deeply significant number twelve. It derives from the movements of our moon, reflected in the monthly life cycle of women, and the fact that in working out one's position at sea, local time is interchangeable with longitude. The phases of the moon and the daily tides, which still regulate business upon the seas, governed the lives of our ancestors.

In the days before street lamps, folk arranged to do their night-time journeys at the time of the full moon. Poachers chose the opposite for obvious reasons. And that is why the moon-dials on grandfather clocks were so important, as well as being a source of visual pleasure, especially to the children of the house. Which nicely introduces my life-long hobby, antiquarian horology.

I bought my first long-case clock in 1957, after I had returned from West Africa. It was a brass-faced eight-day clock made by Daniel Cornwell of Billericay in Essex, and cost £5. Today, it would fetch in the region of £3,000. I became hooked on old clocks and remain so today.

Everyone loves a grandfather clock. As Jane Austen might have said, it is a truth universally acknowledged that every home requires one. And not some reproduction affair, however well made, but an old Georgian or Victorian gentleman who has ticked and struck the hours for perhaps a century and a half or more. And if engraved on its face is some wise maxim exhorting the passer-by to remember the passage of time, why so much the better. Such a clock enhances an old house; without one an ancient hall seems vaguely incomplete. And in an expensive new house, an old mahogany or oak clock will offset the modernity, while in a small one it introduces a reassuring air of dignity.

And what interesting people the old clockmakers were! In their own day, probably the most skilled of the local craftsmen, often with a knowledge of mathematics and astronomy rare in country districts. Many were immigrants, or refugees like the Huguenots, or Jewish craftsmen in Russia, Poland or Germany, fleeing from persecution. And the old newspapers are full of the minutiae of their lives, accidents, scandals, bankruptcies, tragedies, and various infringements of the law, especially illegal pawn-broking, a popular sideline with Jewish members of the trade.

In 1997 I discovered that there was no authoritative book on local clockmakers, so I decided to fill the gap, and doing so wrote my first published book, *Swansea Clocks*. The object was to present a résumé of all the old watch and clockmakers of the area, and their work, but I also had in mind a particular kind of reader, many dozens of whom I have had the good fortune to meet in the course of my research. Owners of clocks are invariably interested in how their clocks work, who made them and when, the kind of people they were, and what their workshops and daily lives were like.

It was not long before I was asked to do my bit for the area by lecturing on Swansea clocks in church halls and village community centres, something I was quite willing to do. Speaking at public meetings holds no terrors for me; any sympathies are better addressed to the audience.

This situation, for which I should apologise, but don't, dates back to my early twenties, when I saw Gabriel Pascal's film production of '*Pygmalion*', and became acquainted with Shaw's immortal dustman, Alfred Dolittle. Mr Dolittle's moving description of the sad condition of the undeserving poor, prompted the distinguished teacher of phonetics, Professor Higgins, to give him a ten pound note. But Alfred refused, asking for a five pound note instead, on the grounds that ten pounds was 'too much to blow in the pub for a night out with my old woman; it made a man feel responsible-like.'

This prompted Higgins to remark to his friend Colonel Pickering: '. . . that if we listen to this man another minute, we won't have a single illusion left.' The sequel was that on Higgins' recommendation, an eccentric American millionaire left Dolittle several thousand pounds a year, on condition he gave one lecture each year on morals. When Higgins's mother asked Dolittle if he was not intimidated by this condition, he replied: 'Intimidated! I'll lecture them until they're blue in the face!' And when I address a meeting this is invariably in my mind.

I have twice been to North America to lecture on Swansea clocks, but the talk I enjoyed most was at the invitation of the Britsh Horological Society in the Linnaean Room in Burlington House, where Charles Darwin first gave his talk of the 'Origin of Species'. I even had his pointing stick in my hand, and was it fancy, but did I feel the dust-laden breath of Alfred Dolittle cheering me on from the dust department of the World to come.

I believe a successful lecturer needs to make the audience laugh. This is never a problem for me; the danger lies in overdoing things, particularly when golden opportunities arise like old men snoring loudly in the front row.

I usually end my clock talks with the following poem, which actually I regard very seriously, for it is how I conduct my life, but it usually raises a laugh as well:

> The clock of Life is wound but once,
> And no man has the power,
> To say just when that clock will stop;
> The day, nor yet the hour.
> This is the only life you have,
> So live it with a will.
> Who knows about tomorrow?
> Those hands may then be still.

My next book was a self-indulgence, but so are they all; I only write them because I am interested in the subject. It was called *Death on Gower*, and with it I ventured into the dubious world of mystery writing. Although it purported to be fiction, and in terms of the plot that is what it was, its purpose was to provide a vehicle for a notional explanation of a mystery in the south of France which had intrigued me for years.

I first read of the mystery of Rennes-le-Château in the mid-eighties, and was intrigued enough to drive down to research it on the spot. The book followed naturally from my fascination with south-west France, and in particular with the land of the Cathars.

France has always been my favourite country to visit; I go there every year, and agree with whoever it was who remarked that all civilised people have two countries; their own, and France.

Collectively, the French do not care for the British, but then neither do they for any other foreigners, and as individuals I find them charming, friendly, and hospitable. I admire and envy their way of life, and spend as much time in their beautiful country as I can. They are not, like us, under the thumbs of our American cousins, and it grieves me to say, when I return from clean, tidy, pleasurable France, bedecked with flowers and vines, I sometimes feel I am returning to the Dark Ages.

Among other things the book occupied three years of agreeable research and reading – that was its attraction – but when it was completed I was not satisfied and put it away in a drawer. Ten years later the idea came to me to re-write it in the first person, making better use of the plot and characters.

There seems little doubt that in the past some degree of danger existed in delving too deeply into the mystery of Rennes-le-Château, and it is my belief that this is still a consideration today. People seem to die suddenly. For example, Bérenger Saunière, the mysterious priest who is at the centre of the mystery, and the three authors of a little book entitled *Le Serpent Rouge*, which was published in 1967. Its contents could be linked to the mystery in vague and ambiguous terms, even though based on dubious sources. Of its three authors, Louis Saint-Maxen and Gaston de Koker were found hanged on the 6th March, 1967, and the next day Pierre Feugere was also discovered hanged, and there were others as well.

The mystery, a genuine, Morocco-bound unsolved enigma, replete with bodies and tales of hidden treasure, begins with the appointment in 1885 of a thirty-year-old Catholic priest named Bérenger Suanière as priest of Rennes-le-Château, one of the many little hill-top villages dotted about the French Pyrenees.

His church was a dilapidated building first consecrated to the Magdalene in 1059, on the site of an earlier Gothic building and his stipend was the equivalent of a few English pounds a year. Probably he would have sometimes gone hungry without having meals in turn with his parishioners.

He was a well educated and studious man, who took a great deal of interest in the history and archaeology of the area, interests he shared with his friend, Henri Boudin, the priest of the neighbouring village of Rennes-les-Bains. In 1887 Saunière began a modest restoration of the interior of his church, limited by available parish funds. Local accounts say that certain old documents were found beneath the altar, at which point he banished the workmen and closed the church for several days. Shortly after this he went to Paris, where he visited St Sulpice, the centre in France for Catholic research into the occult.

There is evidence that while in Paris he made the acquaintance of certain members of Parisian society, including some who were well known to be on the fringes of esoteric circles in the capital, including Emma Calvé, the Maria Callas of her day, and members of the Hapsburg family.

Nothing untoward occurred during the next few years, but in 1895 complaints were made to the Prefect de L'Aude about alleged clandestine activities by Saunière in the church cemetery. But by 1897 things were beginning to happen with a vengeance. Saunière seemed to be receiving money from an unknown source or sources on a large scale and in that year his church was restored in an extraordinary manner, apparently without regard to cost.

Strange almost sinister motifs were incorporated during the refurbishment of the interior. The fourteen stations of the cross, which appear on the walls of all Catholic churches, and as Roman numerals in small churches, were replaced by fourteen specially commissioned and brilliantly executed paintings which run anti-clockwise. Some of the panels incorporated a sly, almost blasphemous departure from the Bible story, although these would not have been apparent to a semi-literate rural congregation, or even to any devout Catholic whose mind was not open to such ideas.

Worse was to come, for Saunière ordered a special statue of the demon Asmodeus, executed in brilliant and striking colours, and complete with a satanic leer, to be set up just inside the church entrance. The figure supported on its head a stoup in the form of a sea-shell – what the superstitious villagers must have thought as their children were baptised in it is hard to imagine. And above the entrance porch he caused the words 'Terrible est Locus iste' to be engraved in the stone.

His spending continued on an increasing scale. Between 1901 and 1905 he bought large plots of land at the top of the village, on which he built the Villa Bethania, a substantial house (which he never occupied), with extensive gardens and a large stone balcony overlooking the valley below. Finally, he added an imposing library tower with a crenellated parapet on the side of the balcony.

Saunière's visitors were scarcely of the type an obscure rural priest would be expected to entertain. They included Emma Calvé – almost certainly one of Saunière's lovers – and others who would certainly not have been approved of in Rome. There were visits from Archduke Johan von Hapsburg, a cousin of the Emperor of Austria, and in due course it emerged that Saunière and the Duke had opened bank accounts on the same day, when large sums were paid to Saunière.

His death was as sensational as his life. Although a hale and hearty man in his mid-sixties he died suddenly in suspicious circumstances. His body was placed, arrayed in his priestly robes in a chair on the balcony, while past it filed a procession of mourners, obviously opulent and from outside the area, each plucking a tassle from his robe. Why?

In 1956, three decaying corpses were discovered in Saunière's garden; had he killed them in self-defence, and secretly disposed of their bodies? These are the essential facts, but they are the tip of an iceberg. Whole shelves of debatable history, pseudo-scientific theories and religious babble-books have been erected upon them. It is strictly nut-case territory, and the fact remains that the mystery of Rennes-le-Château remains as unsolved as ever.

Since writing that book I have been continuing my researches and now realise that the notional theme which provided the basis of my plot, was way off track. Further visits to the area, and something approaching a revelation is tempting me to follow it up with another. But this time it will be a vehicle for what I think might be the real explanation of the mystery, which I now realise is not just centred on Rennes-le-Château, but on its surrounding area. But in the meantime I have other priorities.

Writing fiction, even serious work disguised as fiction, is much harder than straightforward research if you have a complicated plot and numerous characters. But it does have its advantages, the chief of which is that you can put into the mouths of your characters opinions you may not care to admit to yourself. It is courtesan throughout the ages: power without responsibility.

Then followed my *The Swansea Copper Barques and Cape Horners*. In the 19th century, 90% of the world's copper was smelted in Swansea. Its ships and seamen were famous throughout the world, and this book was my tribute to them.

My last book was perhaps – to me at any rate – the most important of all. It was called *The History of the Radio Officer in the Merchant Navy and on Deep-Sea Trawlers* – a long title which alas I could not think of a way of satisfactorily shortening.

The idea of writing it came to me quite suddenly in May 2001 while I was having lunch in the main square of the little hill village of St-Guilhem-le-Désert, near Beziers, in south-west France. Quite extraordinarily, as the reader will have gathered from earlier parts of this book, the subject of this one, so relevant to my own life, had not previously occurred to me. I realise now, that for all sorts of reasons, the time had not been ripe. Then suddenly I realised that this was a task which had to be completed before I could concentrate on anything else.

The Merchant Navy Radio Officer, known to generations of seafarers as 'Sparks', was as integral a part of life on board as the engine room or funnel. He (and later she), provided the link between the ship and the shore, the channel for orders, weather reports, and private messages. And when disaster at sea threatened, was often the only means of attracting help. If the tradition of the sea meant that the Captain was the last to leave his ship, then the Radio Officer was usually the last but one.

The name 'Sparks' was inevitable from the time the first practitioner of the mysterious art of wireless communication at sea thumped away at a Morse key, producing the raspy note and hiss of electrical energy as blue sparks and the smell of ozone radiated from the silver-plated spark gap which lay at the heart of his occult contraption.

Today, the advent of satellite communication, teleprinters and facsimile has rendered the traditional Radio Officer, whose art was based on the Morse Code, as extinct an animal as the brontosaurus. He has passed into marine history along with the lamp-trimmer on a sailing ship or the donkey-man on a steam tramp, taking with him his world of dots and dashes, SOS messages, and telegram forms.

Researching the book for me was an extraordinary experience, for it involved going through a door of forty or more years ago, and meeting old colleagues, friends, and contacts I had never thought to see again. It meant travelling to many of the great ports of the country, meeting people, and researching in local maritime museums. Not only that, because of the wide publicity my research generated, indeed on a global scale, my contacts extended all over the world, particularly in Australia, New Zealand, and North America. The book was honoured by a foreword by His Royal Highness, The Duke of Edinburgh.

These contacts, and the renewal of old friendships have enriched my life, and as I write these words I am awed by the strange workings of fate. Truly, at any stage of one's life, one cannot guess at what may lie ahead. Perhaps it is just as well.

It has occurred to me, now that I have completed this book, that I might spend a year or two wandering about the South Seas, looking, as James Thurber puts it: '. . . silent and inscrutable, like a character in the books of Joseph Conrad.' However, while I might make a good stab at pretending to be inscrutable, I know I could never remain silent – it is not in my nature, unless pressing considerations prevail. So probably I will not do that, and instead spend much more time in south-west France where there is lots of wine and sunshine, and no need at all to be inscrutable.

I suppose at this point I must cease being frivolous, and emerge from the long grass to confess what I have learned. Alas, it is as though I could be listening to Virgil saying to me:

> Where of myself I see no further on,
> I have brought thee hither both by wit and art.
> Take now for they guide thine own heart's pleasure now,
> Forth from the narrows, from the steeps thou art.

But whatever I do there will come the day, when as the old sailors used to say, I will have to let go the mooring, and drift slowly down the Dark River of the Nine Bends. But until then I must decide what to do with what remains of my life.

And if you, dear reader, have stayed with me thus far, I now bid you farewell, and *bon chance*.

Joanna Greenlaw
Swansea
August 2002

INDEX

Amritsar, Punjab, 47
Accra, Nigeria, 55
Baxter, Captain Phillip, 93
Baxtergate, s.s., 89
Bierut, Syria, 52
Buzz-Phrase Generator, 74
Buenos Aires, 110
Calve, Emma, 119
Chabba, Captain Mohan, 43
Cilicia, M.V., Anchor Line, 40
Colombo Amateur Dramatic Society, 49
Corabank, M.V., 94
Cowasjee – Parsee shipowners, Pakistan 50s, 34
Coynant Farm, Llanfynydd, Dyfed, 84
Drupa, M.V., 62
Dyer, General, 47
Edinburgh, HRH The Duke of, 122
Ellis, Captain, 89
Empire Day, 7
Freetown, Sierra Leone, 56
Ghana, 28
'General Orders', 75
Jeremia O'Brien, s.s., 59
Jinnah, 28
Kashmir, 28
Karachi, Pakistan, 33
Kell, Captain Howard, 112
Khan Kalali, Cairo, 61
Kuwait, 62
Kyrenia, Cyprus, 52
Lord Louis Mountbatten, 27
Lagos, Nigeria, 54
Loch Ewe, Scotland, 69
Lorca, s.s., 67
Manningtree, Essex, 80
Marconi, Guglielmo, 72
Marconi International Marine Communication Company Ltd., 72

Marilock, M.V., 42
Mee, Arthur, *Children's Encyclopaedia*, 10
Mistley, Essex, 78
Moriarty, Thomas, from Dingle, Eire, 33
Nacella, M.V., Anglo-Saxon Petroleum Company Ltd., 82
Nehru, 28
Nile Hilton, Cairo, 62
North Anglia, s.s., 108
Ocean Viscount, s.s., 58
Orama, s.s., 20
Parsees, 34
Pentewan, Cornwall, 11
Poplar Farm, Gosbeck, Suffolk, 81
Preston Thomas, 19
Rangoon, Burma, 30
Rennes-le-Château, S.W. France, 118
Romano, Dr, of Palermo, Sicily, 20
Rosario, Argentina, 110
Samdel, s.s., 30
San Nicolas, Argentina, 110
Sherbro, M.V., 53
Shwe Dagon Pagoda, Rangoon, 31
Simpsons in the Strand, 17
Sind Desert, 33
Srinigar, Kashmir, 47
St Austell, Cornwall, 18
Swansea, South Wales, 58
Taj Mahal Hotel, Bombay, 40
Takoradi, Ghana, 54
Tata – Jehanghir Ratanji Dadabhoy, 36
The Swansea Copper Barques and Cape Horners, 59
Toledo, M.V., 35
Waterwitch (Yacht), 83
Welsh Troubadour, M.V., 93
Zorastrianism, 34